# Child's Work
## A Learning Guide to Joyful Play

by Paul S. Shakesby     Edited by Peter J. Dorman

Running Press, Philadelphia

Printed in the United States of America

Distributed in Canada by Van Nostrand Reinhold Ltd., Ontario

Library of Congress Catalog Card Number 7484853

ISBN 0914294172

Art direction, Design and Cover Photography by Jim Wilson
Section and Chapter Head Illustration by Amy Myers
Text Illustration by Laurel Rowlette
Type: Helvetica Light, Composition by Alpha Publications
Cover printed by Pearl Pressman Liberty
Child's Work printed and bound by Port City Press

This book may be ordered directly from the publisher. Please include 25¢ postage.
Try your bookstore first.

Running Press, 38 South Nineteenth Street, Philadelphia, Pennsylvania 19103

# TABLE OF CONTENTS*

*NOTE: Many of the games in these chapters will be enjoyed by children who are somewhat older or younger than the suggested age groupings.

# First Word—An Introduction

## Why Child's Work?

The idea of work means something a little different to each of us. Suppose your child is watching you work. You may be moving a chest, gardening, typing, fixing a flat, or reading. To a young child, your activity might very well be observed as play. We watch our children play—yet our perception does not always correspond with the reality of a child's experience. If we watch closely, we can see more than merely playful diversion. Children involved in their games show evidence of struggle, accomplishment, and defeat. Playing can be hard work for a child. But the difference between a child's work and an adult's is largely one of attitude. Children do not approach their hard-working games with the kind of negativism that our society has conditioned many of us to associate with the idea of work. For the very small people in our world, experience is not so narrowly defined. Let us try to get inside our children's heads, where work can be fun while fun may be work—where playing, working and learning are all one in the same.

## The Parent's Role

In one sense, this is a book about homemade toys which offer sound education as well as good fun and enjoyable work for your child. Yet on another level, the true subject of these pages is the relationship between parent and child. For it is only through your involvement in making the toys and using them with your child that this book will fulfill its purpose. Your preparations and presentations are as much a part of the games as the toys themselves. If you enjoy being with your child, sharing the experiences of learning, growth, and discovery, then you will appreciate the kind of involvement that this book demands. Respect for your child, and for the uniqueness of any parent-child relationship, is a tacit premise underlying all the pages that follow.

# The Plan of The Book

Each chapter aims to accomplish three things: (1) to present a concept in relation to a physical, neurological, or mental facility; (2) to guide you in the construction of a toy or the preparation of a game designed to illustrate that concept; and (3) to describe one or two specific play-exercises, or recommended ways of using the toys. Working through all these play-exercises in order would surely prove to be a broadly fulfilling experience; yet the chapters may well be used independently from one another. There is no strict progression from "easy" to "hard." Almost any chapter will be thoroughly workable apart from the previous ones. Your child's special interests and capabilities should determine where you begin. The arrangement of the chapters into five main parts is intended to give an overview of the contents and the general areas of learning that are explored. Of course, this kind of tight, well-defined structure does not mean to imply any practical distinctions among sensorial, manual, and mental facilities in everyday life.

# Making The Toys

The games, or play-exercises, involve toys that are scientifically sound and educationally constructive. Most of the toys are easily made from common household materials, with the help of simple tools. Cardboard, scrap wood, fabric materials, sandpaper, small jars or bottles, paints, tape, glue, scissors, razor knife, kitchen utensils, common food products, and a variety of objects likely to turn up in the average junk drawer or utility closet—these account for most of the toys described in the book. Whatever is not readily available in your own home may be inexpensively obtained at a crafts or 5 & 10¢ store, a supermarket, hardware or drugstore. Remember that the materials themselves are important: the play-exercises will open your child's eyes to a great variety of materials as well as illustrate the concepts which are built into the proper use of the toys. Yet it must be emphasized that the materials suggested for the games are, in many circumstances, suggestions only. If the principles stated at the beginning of each chapter are followed, the toys which are designed to implement them may be made in a variety of ways, or from a number of possible materials. Putting your own creative imagination to work, you will discover that whatever makes sense and conveys the essential message is appropriate. Thus, apology is now made for the apparent rigidity of some of the toy-making instructions. It would be awkward to suggest all the reasonable alternatives in every variable circumstance. Let these chapters serve to guide you in the best possible use of your skills, ideas, and resources.

# Doing The Exercises

A similar approach should be taken to the play-exercises themselves. The activities suggested in the chapters represent the most obvious and immediate ways of working with your materials. A little imagination will go a long way in putting the toys to new and various uses. Your child will surely be the instigator of many other extraordinary applications. Most children under ten years of age will be stimulated by a great majority of these toys. The age-groupings specified in the **Table of Contents** merely suggest a time period when your child is likely to be most sensitive to a particular toy or game. Remember that a child should progress with, and benefit from, each play-exercise according to his or her own unique rate of development. While some of the games can be completed in a single sitting, many are really long-term projects that will continue to entertain an enlighten your child for weeks or months on end. This is especially true of the exercises involving language and numbers. But not even the simplest game is ever really completed for the inquisitive and open-minded child. Over the months and years your child will be able to return to them again and again, each time with new perceptions and heightened sensitivities. The book itself is kinetic: it will grow with your child and its usefulness will change as your child changes.

# The Montessori Factor

The basic philosophy of a Montessori classroom involves progressive learning through manipulation. Materials and toys are made to accomodate to the size and physical capabilities of the child. Most toys are conceived as the vehicles for teaching one specific concept at a time. Games are designed to stimulate neurological development and make the child aware of her or his actual and potential growth. The Montessori method encourages a system of learning concepts through calculated progressions. While some of the tenets of this method are preserved in this book, there is also considerable departure. In **Child's Work** learning occurs through the special relationship between parent and child, a kind of one-to-one rapport which is difficult to achieve in a classroom situation. Because the toys will not be used by large groups of children, they do not have to be as durable as the expensive, precision-made models found in the schools. So, along with the satisfaction derived from making your own toys are the added attractions of simple constructions at a very low cost. Moreover, most of the toys described in this book, unlike some of those used in the Montessori system, are designed for dual or multiple purposes. While each play-exercise presents one main concept, you will see how secondary concepts are suggested or advanced during the games. And because these games do not follow a tight, systematic progression, they allow your child to pursue special interests and a natural course of development.

8

# A Note on Gender

Many of us, by now, are tired of hearing our little girls referred to as "he" or "him." Presumably, about half the readers of this book might at one time or another share this feeling. In a book of this type, relating as it does to the formative stages of child development, it is especially important to be aware of the attitudes generated through linguistic implication. It just seems wrong that writers should continue to resist any effort to acknowledge fully the female identity. To be sure, our grammatical system is rigid and biased, and the attempt to pay due respect to both sexes usually leads to awkward wordiness. This book does not propose any grammatical revolution, except to say that it is concerned with boys and girls together, and wishes not to conceal that concern. Accordingly, half the chapters, on an alternating basis, speak of the "him" who is your child; the other half speak of the "her." It is hoped that the reader's ear will become as accustomed to these alternating references as it has been to the established, unfaltering usage of the male pronouns. In **Child's Work**, the flip of a coin determined whether the first chapter, and subsequently odd-numbered chapters, should use the male or female reference. Heads, she; tails, he.

Peter J. Dorman

# Part I: Sensorial Awareness

The first seven chapters of **Child's Work** describe home-made games which are designed to exercise and refine your child's sensorial responsiveness. Hearing, smelling, seeing, tasting, and touching are, of course, the senses involved. Discovering the finer grades of distinction within each kind of sensorial stimulus will be a thoroughly enjoyable and broadening experience.

# Chapter 1: Sound Bottles

Your child can have a lot of fun while discovering different tonal qualities in the sound bottles. Small jars are used to contain various granular substances. When shaken, each jar will sound at a certain pitch, according to the properties of the materials within each glass. The play-exercises develop your child's sense of hearing in a simple and entertaining way.

PREPARING THE SOUND BOTTLES. Ten small-size baby food bottles and their tops will do well. To keep the game purely auditory, the bottled materials should not be seen. Use enamel paint to make the glass opaque. Five bottles (including tops) should

Fig. 1

| ORANGE | ORANGE | ORANGE | ORANGE | ORANGE |
|--------|--------|--------|--------|--------|
| YELLOW | YELLOW | YELLOW | YELLOW | YELLOW |

be painted, inside and out, with one color, perhaps orange; the other five may be painted yellow. Have some white glue available for later use. When the paint is dry, you are ready to introduce the five noise-making materials. Small quantities of sand, hard lentils, wooden or plastic beads, rice, and tiny pebbles are suggested. Prepare a set of five orange bottles and five yellow, making each container about ⅛ full: one yellow bottle and one orange bottle for the rice, one yellow and one orange for the pebbles, etc., until there are five pairs of different noise-making containers. (See Fig.1.)

Before gluing on the tops to seal the contents of the bottles, two details must be checked. First, listen to verify that the two members of each pair sound the same when shaken gently. Then, using one colored set of bottles, listen to verify that five different sounds are actually produced. If, for instance, your rice and lentils sound the same, or near enough to create ambiguity, remove the rice from both the rice bottles and try using raisins. You may wish to experiment with several substitute substances. For the purpose of checking error during the exercises, it might be helpful to label the bottles before sealing them. Do this by sticking a very small piece of tape, with an identifying code number, on the underside of the bottles. When all the sounds have been tested, showing that they are

13

distinct in the yellow bottles and matching with the sounds in the orange bottles, secure the painted tops to the bottle necks by applying glue to both surfaces.

HEARING THE TONES. Your child's sensitivity to the five different tones can be exercised in several ways. First, use just one set of five bottles to make a sequence of the sounds from high to low. You must begin by differentiating between high and low. Gently shake the bottle that makes the highest pitch and tell your child, "this is the highest sound." Shake the bottle of the opposite extreme and say, "this is the lowest sound." Ask you child to shake the bottles and reproduce these sounds by herself. Now illustrate with a medium-pitch sound. When she grasps the idea of distinction between high, middle, and low sounds, demonstrate with all five bottles, and then let your child try it. Have her now experiment with all the bottles and arrange them in order from high to low. You might also ask her to try a soft-to-loud sequence: the sand makes the soft sound, the pebbles a loud sound.

All ten bottles may now be used for a pairing, or matching game. Your child simply finds the corresponding sounds from the two colored sets of bottles and pairs them. Each yellow bottle should be placed with its orange counterpart. Check her matchings either by listening or by the code on the bottom, if you have decided to use one. Another exercise demonstrates that the noise produced by any bottle can vary according to the way it is shaken. Start with a gentle shaking action and proceed to a vigorous one. Ask your child to close her eyes and determine whether you are shaking slowly or fast merely by listening to the sounds. Using these sound bottles, you may devise a variety of exciting and challenging games for your child. It is always interesting to apply the lessons of these play-exercises to the spontaneous happenings in your everyday environment. See if your child can recognize the various tones produced by the radio, the horn of the car, people's voices, etc. The two suggested games in this chapter—perceiving a sequence and matching like with like—are basic kinds of exercises used with many of the materials in this book.

# Chapter 2: Olfactory Containers

Children, at a young age, do not consciously know that they can smell. The ability to distinguish smells is a talent that children are amazed to discover they possess. Merely drawing their attention to odors provides little new awareness: the child intuits an experience of smell, but lacks the awareness of that experience. The smelling exercise cultivates a discriminating responsiveness to olfactory stimuli, and helps the child to recognize that specific odors are generated by specific substances.

PREPARING THE CANNISTERS. Ten small medicine bottles (spice jars, or the like), five of them dark green and five dark brown, may be used as the olfactory cannisters for the smelling games. These bottles should be of one or two fluid ounce capacity. Also procure ten easy-fitting corks and a box of cotton balls. Five odoriferous materials that can either fit into the cannisters or be absorbed by the cotton are necessary. This exercise uses pure lemon extract in liquid form, mint leaves, perfumed soap, liquid disinfectant, and malt vinegar.

Preparation for the play-exercise involves odorizing each of the green bottles—and likewise each of the brown—with one of the five scented materials. First, pour a few drops of lemon extract on six or eight cotton balls. Push half of these into one green bottle, the other half into a brown one. Cork them shut. Do the same with the malt vinegar and the disinfectant liquid. Shred enough of the mint leaves to cover the bottoms of two bottles (a green and a brown). Insert the scented shreddings and cover them in their cannisters with three or four cotton balls to absorb and concentrate the diffusing odors. Likewise, prepare a green and a brown cannister with shredded soap. Do not forget the corks. Now you have five different pairs of scented cannisters. (See Fig. 2.)

GREEN MINT LEAVES

LAVENDER SOAP BALLS

LEMON EXTRACT DISINFECTANT MALT VINEGAR

Fig. 1

THE SMELLING GAME. The two-part
exercise is elementary and enlightening.
Your child will learn to identify and name
each odor, and then to pair the scented
brown bottles with the corresponding green
ones.

**Fig. 2**
LEMON DISINFECTANT VINEGAR MINT SOAP

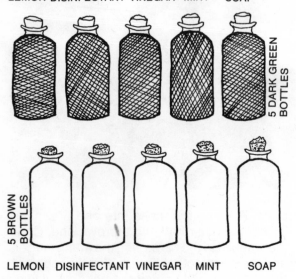

5 DARK GREEN BOTTLES

5 BROWN BOTTLES

LEMON DISINFECTANT VINEGAR MINT SOAP

Begin by showing your child how to
remove a cork carefully and replace it
snugly. Precision of movement is important
to illustrate that care must be taken during
the activity. Uncork the green cannisters and
indicate the difference between each smell.
When you sniff the first bottle exaggerate the
sniffing action. (It may be helpful first to
disturb the air by blowing into the bottle.)
Name the odors: "This is the lemon odor.
Can you smell the lemon odor?" Allow your
child to master perhaps three of the smells
before moving on to the others. Let him cork
and uncork the bottles himself. This is an
important part of the exercise. It shows that
odors can be contained, or hidden from the
senses.

The next part of the smelling game
involves pairing the odors in the green
bottles with the same odors in the brown.
Again, begin with two or three pairs and
progress from there. Say, for instance, "can
you put the two lemon odors together? Now
can you match the other odors"? Have your
child attempt these matchings with his eyes
closed or blindfolded.

16

# Chapter 3: Color Cards and Solutions

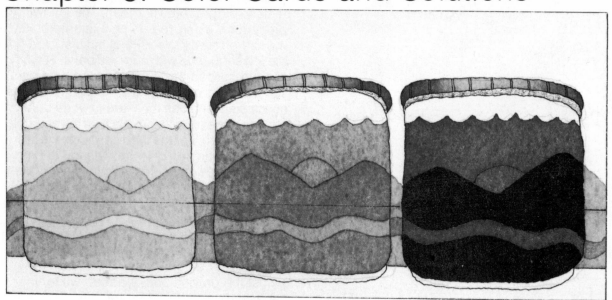

The play-exercises in this chapter invite your child to explore the realm of colors by developing her awareness of their physical and aesthetic properties. Your child may learn the difference between primary and secondary colors, and how to blend and create new colors from the primary red, yellow, and blue. She may learn, moreover, to discriminate among various color shadings, and come to understand what is meant by relatively dark or light tints of a given color. What follows is a systematic approach to the experience of color by working with small, variously painted cards, and with bottles containing translucent solutions of food coloring in water.

MAKING THE COLOR CARDS. To make the color cards you will need one piece of cardboard, at least 10"x 10", and nine colors of paint—red, blue, yellow, green, brown, white, purple, pink, orange (enamels are preferable, but water colors are less expensive). Divide the cardboard into 50 rectangular sections, each measuring 1"x 2" (Fig. 1). Cut out the individual cards, of which only 46 will be needed. From these 46 sections, three groups of color cards will be made (although you may choose to make each group as your child progresses with the exercises).

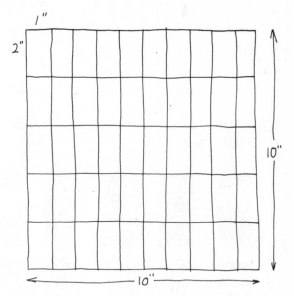

Fig. 1

Group I (6 cards). Primary colors: Paint two cards each of red, yellow, and blue. (See Fig. 2.)

Group II (16 cards). Primary, secondary, and other colors: Paint two cards each of red, yellow, blue, orange, green, purple, brown, and pink. (See Fig. 2.)

## Fig. 2

RED     BLUE     YELLOW

**GROUP I**

RED     BLUE     PINK     BROWN

YELLOW     ORANGE     GREEN     PURPLE

**GROUP II**

**Group III** (24 cards). Six different colors presented in four shades of each, illustrating

a dark-to-light gradation: Obtain the various tints by blending white paint with red, blue, yellow, purple, brown, green. The following procedure, using red as an example color, works well (see Fig. 3). Paint the first card in the red sequence with pure red paint. For the second card in the red sequence, use the same amount of red paint as for the first card, now mixed with one measure of white paint: one measure of white equals ⅓ of the amount of original red. For the third card, mix the red with two measures of white. The fourth card contains three measures of white; hence this card, containing three units of each color, will be half white and half red. Similarly, tint the other five colors, yielding four phases of a dark-to-light sequence. Since commercial paint products will vary, test the mixtures on scrap paper before painting the cards: adjust the proportions of added white, if necessary, in order to guarantee a distinguishable difference among all four tints.

PREPARING THE COLOR SOLUTIONS. Obtain three baby food jars (3-4 oz), or the like, and remove all paper labels from them. Introduce some red food coloring in one, blue in another, and yellow in the third (Fig. 4). Add enough water to make the solutions sufficiently translucent for you to see your

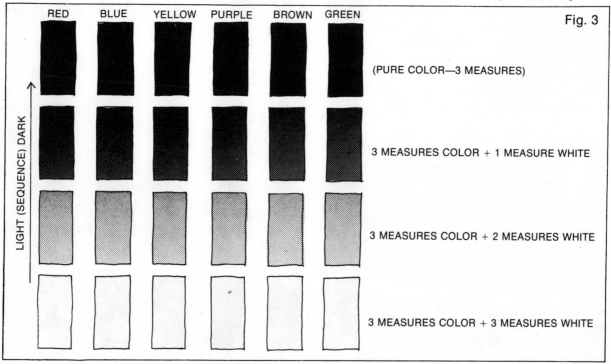

Fig. 3

RED    BLUE    YELLOW    PURPLE    BROWN    GREEN

LIGHT (SEQUENCE) DARK

(PURE COLOR—3 MEASURES)

3 MEASURES COLOR + 1 MEASURE WHITE

3 MEASURES COLOR + 2 MEASURES WHITE

3 MEASURES COLOR + 3 MEASURES WHITE

18

fingers through the jars as you hold them; but not so much as to dilute the vividness of the colors.

Fig. 4

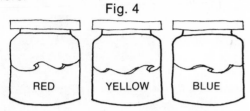

RED   YELLOW   BLUE

DISCOVERING AND EXPLORING THE COLORS. Begin with the primary color cards from Group I (use perhaps only two colors for a very young child). A methodical system of teaching the names of the colors will hold your child's interest. Say, for example, "this is the red card," and "this is the blue card." Let her examine the colors. Then say, "show me the blue card," or "show me the red card." When she can identify them in this manner, point to the blue card and ask, "which one is this?" This basic, three-step method is effective and stimulating for your child: (1) this is the blue; (2) show me the blue; (3) which one is this? (pointing). The three-point system for learning names has been used with great success by Montessorians.

Pairing the reds, yellows, and blues is the next phase of these play-exercises. Simply mix the six cards from Group I and ask your child to put the two of each color together. You may at this time find it appropriate to mention that these three are called the "primary" colors, and that other colors are made from them. Do not hesitate to use the proper scientific terms with your child. She will not know that they are "scientific."

The cards in Group II show eight different colors—the three primary, three secondary (green = yellow + blue; purple = red + blue; orange = yellow + red), and pink and brown. Teach the names of the five new colors in the manner suggested above. Of course, it may require a long period of time for your child to identify consistently these colors by their names. But even before she can do this, she should be able to match the eight color pairs from a scrambled heap of sixteen cards. To reinforce her previous learning, you may ask her to separate the primary colors from the others. Refer to the others as "secondary" colors (although

brown and pink are not technically so-called), and mention that green, for example, is composed of yellow and blue. The idea of combining colors to create new ones can be vividly illustrated with the jars of color solutions.

These jars are translucent and transparent, so that objects seen through them will appear to be colored like the solution. Ask your child to close or cover one eye and view different objects in her environment through a colored bottle. Using these bottles, she can now observe the formation of secondary colors. If she looks through the blue and yellow bottles, held together before her eye, she will see green. Ask her to hold up other combinations of bottles in order to discover orange and purple. You may further demonstrate the formation of secondary colors by mixing small amounts of any two primary solutions in a clear glass. Making new colors in this way will be a wonderful game for your child. Continue adding small amounts of water to these solutions to show how a dark color can be made lighter.

A pink card from Group II can be used also to introduce the idea of different shades of color. One of the lighter shades in the red sequence of the Group III cards will closely resemble this original pink card. Explain to your child that pink is a lighter shade of red. Tell her how you made these variously tinted cards, and ask if she can see the difference in the four shades of each color. You may approach the Group III exercises by aligning the color sequences in columns from dark to light, as in Figure 3. Indicate the color at the top of each column and explain the difference in tints by using the terms **dark, darker, darkest,** and **light, lighter, lightest.** Show her a dark green card, a lighter one, an even lighter one, and finally the lightest. Be sure that she does not mistake **dark** or **light** for the names of these tints: emphasize that these terms serve only to compare one color with another. Many challenging and exciting games can be devised with the color cards and color jars. The play-exercises described here will surely provide your child with weeks and weeks of joyful enlightenment.

# Chapter 4: Taste Bottles

Different areas of the tongue are sensitive to different tastes. The taste bottles are used in exercises that enable your child to experience and differentiate the four basic taste sensations. The front tip of the tongue contains the buds that are sensitive to a **sweet** taste. A **salty** or **sour** taste is perceived along the sides and edges of the tongue. The back, central area is receptive to **bitter** sensations. The central top part of the tongue is not sensitive to any particular tastes. Figure 1 indicates taste location in the tongue.

solutions of the basic taste stimulants. Obtain some brown sugar for the sweet taste, table salt for the salty tast, lemon juice (or vinegar) for the sour taste, and bittersweet baking chocolate (or cocoa) for the bitter taste. These foods must be diluted in

Fig. 2

BABY FOOD BOTTLES    4 OZ. SIZE

Fig. 1
TONGUE

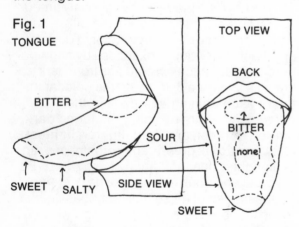

PREPARING THE TASTE BOTTLES. Four baby food jars (approx. 4 oz. size), with their labels removed, will be used to contain lukewarm water to avoid overwhelming your child's sensitivity. Filling the bottles halfway with warm water, prepare four different solutions by dissolving ¼ teaspoon of salt; ½ teaspoon of sugar; 5 or 6 drops of lemon juice; and a few dark, chocolate chips. The best prepared solutions—which you yourself should sample—will have a sufficient hint of taste without leaving a strong after-taste that might modify the effect of the next solution.

STIMULATING THE TASTE BUDS. Now you are ready to present the four taste bottles to your child for experimentation. Line them up and explain that each bottle contains a basic kind of taste which he is used to from many foods and drinks. Explain that the tongue contains tiny taste buds which receive the different tastes, just as the ear receives sound. You may use Figure 1—perhaps demonstrate with your own tongue or his—to show how different areas of the tongue are sensitive to different kinds of tastes. Begin, now, to test each area for its sensitivity. Dip a teaspoon into the sugar solution and have your child taste it with the tip of his tongue. Using a clean spoon for each taste, have him stimulate each area of the tongue with a different solution. He should be able to learn the name of each taste, and differentiate among the sensations, without much difficulty.

It is advisable to make fresh solutions each time you begin these play-exercises. As a variation on the tasting-game, prepare a second set of four taste bottles with the same ingredients as the first four. Ask your child to pair the two sour tastes, the two sweets, etc. Later, when he is readily familiar with all the terms, your child will surely enjoy trying to identify the basic taste of some common foods: honey, beets (sweet); pickles, rhubarb (sour); olives, potato chips (salty); coffee, cinnamon (bitter). Perhaps you might also like to expalin to your child that **smelling** helps him to become aware of the taste of foods. Have him squeeze his nostrils while taking in some food and notice the absence of any definite taste sensation. With the nose pinched, a piece of apple is indistinguishable from a slice of raw potato.

# Chapter 5: White Powders

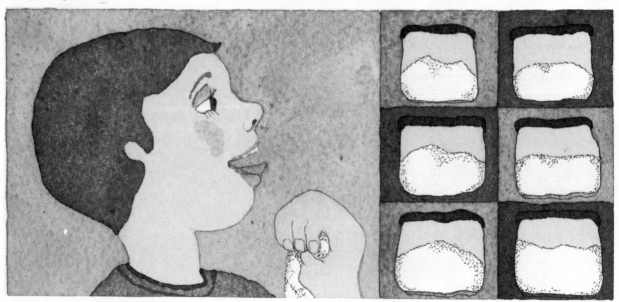

In these play-exercises your child will face the challenge of discriminating among various powdered substances that appear to be quite similar. The task of identifying the powders will excite her inherent sense of inquisitiveness. The experience of discovering that appearances may be deceptive will come alive as six common kitchen products are used to stimulate your child's senses of touch and taste. While a close-up look at the six white powders will also help her to differentiate among them,

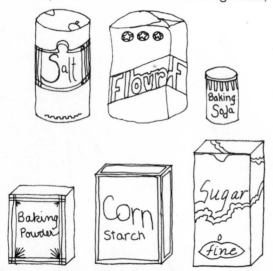

the emphasis in these exercises should not be placed too heavily on visual perception. The overall purpose is basically twofold:

neurologically, to cultivate further the tactile and gustatory senses; and, practically, to reveal that baking soda, for example, is quite different from the several products which from a distance may all seem to be alike.

SETTING UP THE POWDERS. Flour, salt, white sugar, cornstarch, baking powder, and baking soda are the substances to be explored and identified. Half fill each of six baby food jars (or similar containers, about 3 oz. capacity) with one of the powders and write the name of the ingredient on a gummed label or piece of tape (Fig. 1). Do the same with six other jars, but leave these unlabeled. Make sure you have lids for all twelve containers. For the sake of neatness,

Fig. 1

SUGAR  SALT  BAKING POWDER

BAKING SODA  FLOUR  CORN STARCH

place these containers on a tray and have a few paper towels available.

22

IDENTIFYING THE WHITE POWDERS.
These play-exercises will be described in terms of the six powders suggested above; of course, you may use similar substitutes, or fewer powders, depending on their availability in your household. Note for yourself that sugar and cornstarch represent perhaps the two extremes with regard to texture, taste, and appearance. The sweet sugar is composed of crystals that contrast sharply with the neutral tasting, finely powdered cornstarch. If you are using unbleached flour, observe that it is not so purely white and finely powdered as bleached flour.

Fig. 2

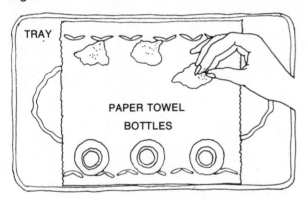

Begin with the labeled bottles, three at a time (or two for younger children). Show your child the containers of sugar, baking soda, and flour. Explain that these ingredients are very different from each other, even though they look alike. In fact, she can **feel** the differences among them. First spoon out a small amount of sugar on a paper towel, and feel its crystals by manipulating your thumb, middle, and index fingers around them (Fig. 2). Now have your child feel the sugary texture, and ask her if she can see the tiny, slightly glossy, crystals. Next, observe the fine, distinctive texture of the baking soda, and compare this with a small amount of flour placed on the paper towel a few inches from the other heaps (Fig. 2). The flour is somewhat rougher (especially if unbleached) than the baking soda, but much smoother than the sugar. Be sure to emphasize the names of these powders as you point them out. By touching the tip of her index finger to each of the substances, your

child may now begin to explore their tastes. The sugar is distinctly sweet; the flour has a neutral taste, with a hint of sweetness; and the baking soda creates a tangy, effervescent sensation on the tongue.

Now spoon out small amounts of the other powders, one at a time, next to the first three heaps on the paper towel. Explore and discover the salt, cornstarch, and baking powder for their tactile and gustatory properties. The baking powder is composed of smooth, tiny granules having a bittery sharp, acidic taste. The cornstarch, a very fine powder, has a neutral taste. The salt crystals, slightly larger than the sugar crystals but not as glossy, have, of course, the familiar salty taste.

When your child is accustomed to the names and properties of the various white powders, clean up the tray and introduce the six unlabeled bottles. Ask her to examine their ingredients and match them with those in the labeled containers. The salt and sugar should be the easiest to match, while the other four may present a real challenge. Finally, you may dispense with the labeled bottles altogether. Using touch and taste, and whatever help visual examination may afford, your child may attempt to identify the contents of the six unmarked bottles.

# Chapter 6: Baric, Thermal, & Touch Tablets

The baric, thermal, and touch tablets are small, rectangular slabs made from materials which exercise your child's sensitivity to weight (baric), heat, and surface texture. These sensitivities will be explored with respect to the differing physical properties of four common materials: clay (plasticine), wood, carpet padding, and styrofoam. There should be eight tablets—four identical pairs—all the same size and all in their natural colors. Similarity in size and lack of vivid coloration will minimize the visual attractiveness of the pieces. Hence the child can learn to experience differentation among objects apart from his most usual way of doing so—with the eye.

MAKING THE TABLETS. The tablets should all be made 3″ x 1½″. Their thickness should approximate ¼″. (See Fig. 1.) The two styrofoam tablets can accurately be cut to size with a razor knife, and then a kitchen knife for slicing them to the proper thickness. A coping saw, with the help of a vise, should be sufficient for the wood, preferably ¼″ plywood. Rough, splintery edges should be smoothed down with sandpaper. Any scrap of neutral-colored carpet padding should be cut with a good scissors or razor knife. The clay (5 & 10¢ store plasticine) can be made

to the prescribed size by rolling out a piece about ¼″ thick and four inches square (or larger). Use a sharp knife to cut the two rectangular tablets from this larger piece. The plasticine can be given added rigidity, if desired, by slipping two ice cream sticks inside its length. With their natural textures preserved, these tablets should remain aesthetically pleasing to the feel.

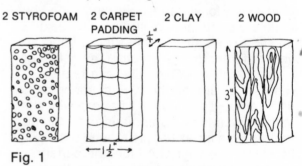

2 STYROFOAM   2 CARPET PADDING   2 CLAY   2 WOOD

**Fig. 1**

CULTIVATING THE SENSES. By developing your child's non-visual, sensorial awareness of the qualities of various materials, these play-exercises will heighten his concentration and increase his span of attention. For a child less than six years old (and for yourself as well), the tactile, thermal, and baric exercises can be performed and learned with greater ease if they are started by first examining the two extreme tablets, the clay and the styrofoam.

24

Once the largest discrepancies are perceived, the subtler ones introduced by the other tablets will be more apparent. Becoming aware of these distinctions is a learning process that even adults may well have to re-examine.

The first exercise is baric, exploring sensitivity to differentiation in weight. Randomly place four different tablets on a table. Show your child the plasticine tablet and tell him that it is the heaviest one. Give it to him to "feel" the heavy clay. Then show him the lightest one, the styrofoam, and tell him it is the lightest. Let him experience its lightness. Now demonstrate with the wood, the second heaviest tablet; and finally the padding, heavier than the styrofoam but lighter than the wood and clay. When your child is familiar with their relative weights, you may ask him to align the tablets in order from heavy to light.

Now he is ready to begin matching the pairs by weight. Mix all eight tablets on the table. Ask your child to determine which ones weigh the same by holding any tablet in one hand and, one at a time, picking up the others for comparison. This should be done by trial and error until he has found the one of similar weight. Continue this game until all eight tablets are successfully paired.

The thermal exercise follows the same general course as the baric. Each of the materials absorbs and radiates a certain amount of heat. Try for yourself to experience how much heat the clay draws from your fingers. The tablet feels cold to the touch. The wood is less cold. The carpet padding feels almost neutral (relative to your own body heat). And the styrofoam, which has different thermal properties, feels somewhat warm. Now have your child feel the clay and tell him it is cold. Do the same with the other tablets while describing the heat quality. Point out that the wood is almost as cold as the clay, while the carpet and styrofoam are not. The activity can be completed by grading the four tablets in a sequence from cold to warm. Also follow the baric exercise by pairing the tablets with the same thermal quality.

The touch exercise illustrates differentiation among surface textures. Experiencing such tactile awareness requires more concentration than the other two exercises and relies on the finer, more sensitive use of the fingers. But children are apt to be more sensitive to those fine distinctions which adults, in their haste, often overlook. You may characterize the surface textures with such words as smooth, slippery, rough, soft, coarse, hard, light, (less smooth, harder), etc. Have your child run two or three fingers along the four different surfaces and become aware of their distinctive feels. Pairing and matching the eight tablets according to texture should be the next step in the exercise.

Game-playing with the tablets can be made more fun and even more educational by the use of a blindfold. Your child may experience an increased sensitivity to the materials while doing the exercises with the awareness that no amount of visual aid is necessary for success. If your child should be reluctant to have his eyes covered, he may prefer to have the tablets put in a dark, cloth bag (large enough for your own hands to move about in comfortably). Using the bag or the blindfold, your child may try pairing two of the eight tablets according to either baric, thermal, or tactile quality. (If a bag is used, the exercise should be done with both hands in it.) After a pairing has been made, it may be verified by removing the blindfold or removing the two tablets from the bag; let your child now see the pieces. If the match is correct, one of the pair should be placed aside on the table and its mate be returned to the other group of six. This process goes on until four different tablets are placed aside on the table, leaving the other set of four to remain together.

# Chapter 7: Fabric Collection

The fabric collection is used in a familiarizing exercise designed to allow children to become aware of the sensitivity they possess in their tiny fingertips. Because the textural distinctions among the several fabrics are much finer than those in the four touch tablets, the following tactile game allows for visual observation to assist in identifying the materials and to provide for a control of error.

CHOOSING THE FABRICS. To present the play-exercise you will need to choose five or six different fabrics which show a distinct textural gradation from rough to smooth. It is necessary to have one soft, smooth material, such as silk, and one very coarse material like burlap. The following fabrics, which you may obtain from old clothes or scrap materials, are listed in a rough-to-smooth sequence: burlap, terry cloth, tweed, wool, velvet, corduroy, linen, cotton flannel, nylon, silk, satin. (This sequence is generally accurate, though it may vary somewhat according to the weave of the specific fabric.) Linen is a good example of a texture intermediate between burlap and silk. It is important also that the fabrics you choose be of contrasting color patterns. Make two small pieces of each fabric, cutting the five materials you use into 4″ squares. Finally,

obtain a pull-string bag, in which two adult hands can fit easily and move comfortably.

FEELING THE MATERIALS. The differences in color pattern as well as texture

Fig. 1

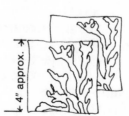

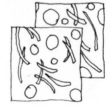

SQUARES OF FABRICS IN PAIRS
— DIFFERENT PATTERNS

4″ approx.

26

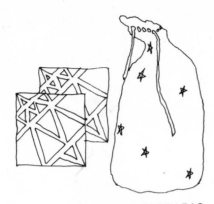

PULL-STRING CLOTH BAG

will initially help your child to identify the fabrics, and later provide a control to ensure that the exercise has been done correctly. For the first demonstration, pick out the two pairs of fabrics that offer the most contrast in texture. Using one from each pair, demonstrate by feeling the pieces with two fingers and a thumb. Before comparing them, feel out each material individually for its own textural value. Then, with burlap or terry cloth, contrast the texture of silk or satin by feeling and saying, "this fabric feels coarse, and that fabric feels soft—see if you can feel the difference." Then add a piece of intermediate texture (linen, perhaps) and demonstrate the different textures of all three fabrics. Continue adding materials until your child is familiar with five fabrics. Some words that are helpful in describing the various textures are rough, coarse, fuzzy, scratchy, hairy, ridged, nubby (linen), soft, smooth, flimsy, slick.

When your child is familiar with the feels of the different fabrics, place them with their matching pieces into the cloth bag. Now have her match the pairs by feeling within the bag. After each matching, take out the pair to check visually. You may vary the game by asking your child to take out the softest fabric, or the roughest. If she has difficulty, limit the contents of the bag to two or, perhaps, three different pairs. Older children should have less difficulty. When she is confident with this activity, add to the bag as many pairs as she can cope with. Teach the names of the fabrics and then ask her to identify the fabrics by name from within the bag. She can always check visually when the materials are removed.

# Part II: Manual Dexterity

In the play-exercises from Part II, your child will work at some everyday, practical activities. At the same time he will become aware of the importance of properly using his hands to accomplish little tasks. Developing the manual skills involved in these tasks provides a practical foundation for several of the exercises later in the book; although those chapters may be explored beforehand, if your child is already fairly adept.

# Chapter 8: Sorting Grains

The first exercise involving a controlled and deliberate use of the hand will be a delightful game for your child. As in all the exercises that stress manual dexterity, the dexterity itself is a means to an end. Here, the point of the game is to show that grains which have been mixed together can be separated again. Brown rice and table salt are the grains commonly used. The mixture can be sorted into its components by using a sieve which allows only the salt to pass through.

SETTING UP THE GAME. Besides the two boxes of grains (salt and rice), you will need two small bowls (cereal or soup bowls), two small cylindrical containers or food jars, and a food strainer, or sieve, smaller in diameter than the bowls, and permitting only the salt to sift through. Also, obtain a tray, large enough to accomodate all the materials, and a small whisk broom to brush up spills.

SORTING THE GRAINS. The sorting exercise is performed directly on the tray. With very deliberate movements, to emphasize each step, pour brown rice into one container until it is half full. Pour the same amount of salt into the other container. Show your child the different grains in the separate containers and tell him that you are going to mix them in one of the bowls. First pour the rice into a bowl, and then pour in the

salt. Gently shake the bowl with the salt and rice to ensure their mixing. Now, show your child the proper way of holding a sieve. Essentially, it is grasped with three fingers around its handle and the palm in an up-position. See Figure 1. It does not have to be squeezed tightly; the stem of the sieve rests gently under the palm. Pour the mixture into the sieve, held over the second bowl. As you shake the sieve gently but deliberately, notice that the lateral movement can be totally controlled with the first three fingers; the fourth and fifth fingers are not essential. The salt strains into the bowl, while the rice remains in the sieve. Now you have demonstrated how a mixture of grains can be separated into its components.

Show your child that the exercise is not complete until the materials are returned, neatly, to the proper places. The salt from the bowl and the rice from the sieve should be carefully poured back into the containers. Any spilled grains should be whisked into a bowl, sifted, and returned to their respective containers. Now let your child play the game. Remind him, if necessary, of the steps of the exercise. Let him pour the grains into the containers, mix them in one bowl, and sift them through the sieve into the second bowl. Make sure he is holding the sieve comfortably and with control. When he is finished tidying up, the materials may be left on the tray for the next time your child wants to sort grains.

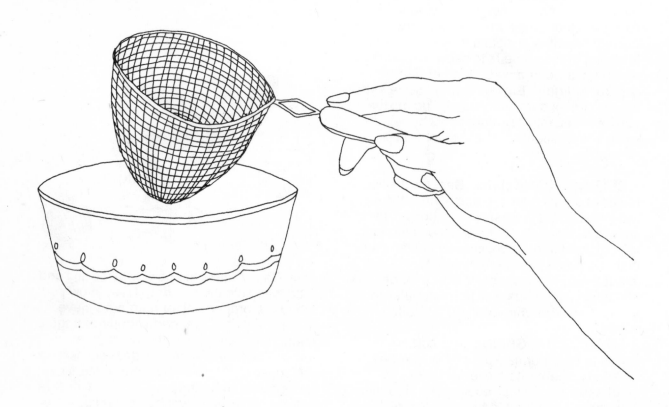

# Chapter 9: Cardboard Rectangles With Knobs

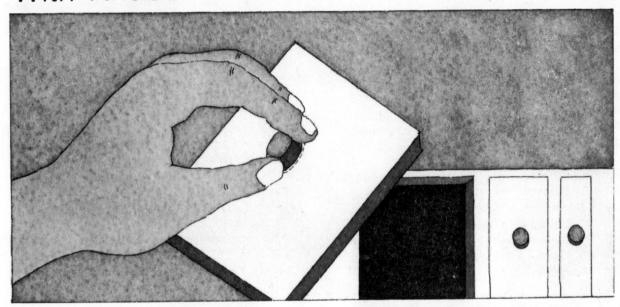

Humans possess a highly specialized facility for manipulating small objects with the use of their thumb, index, and middle fingers. While this facility will develop naturally on its own, your child can derive much satisfaction and enhance her manual dexterity by consciously exercising the "three-finger sense" at a young age. Dexterity in the coordination of these fingers will enable her more readily to hold a pencil correctly, to operate handles and knobs, to pick up objects, and manipulate tools. The toy in this chapter is designed primarily to exercise this dexterity. The play-exercises will further build upon the concept of ordered sequence, and at the same time develop your child's sense of hand-and-eye coordination. Here she will work with five rectangular cardboard cut-outs, varying in size, each one fitted to a rectangular slot in a cardboard frame. The pieces are manipulated by small, wooden knobs glued to their surfaces.

MAKING THE TOY. The toy consists of a large, rectangular frame, from which five smaller rectangles are cut out (see Fig. 1). These pieces are the insets, which vary in an ordered sequence from 3″ x 3″ to 1″ x 3″. You

Fig. 1   TOP VIEW

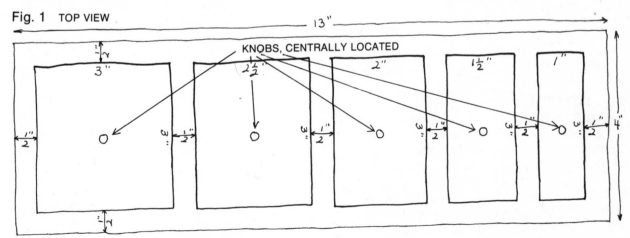

will need some heavy cardboard (carton thickness), a razor knife, glue, ruler, and a short piece of wooden dowel (about ⅜" diameter) for making the knobs. Carefully cut the cardboard into two pieces, measuring 4" x 13" each. On one piece, diagram the five smaller rectangles according to the dimensions indicated in Figure 1. Note that there is a uniform, ½" margin all around the frame, and a ½" space between each of the insets. Use a straightedge and razor knife to cut out the five pieces. The cut-out frame which remains should be pasted to the other piece of 4" x 13" cardboard, providing a solid backing for the insets. On each of the five cut-outs that you now have, glue a short piece (about ⅜" - ½") of wooden dowel, sanded smoothly, to serve as a knob. (See Fig. 2). You may wish to paint the frame and insets to make a more durable and attractive toy.

WORKING WITH THE INSETS. Begin with the five pieces set into their corresponding frames. Show your child the proper way of holding the knob with her first three fingers. (These tiny knobs, of course, will be much

Fig. 2
INSETS AND FRAMES

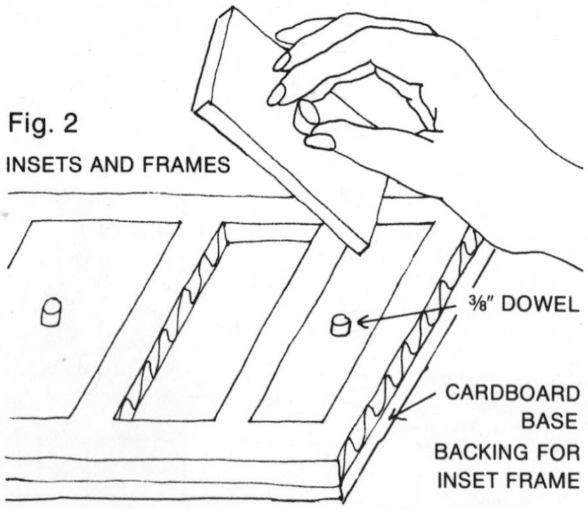

⅜" DOWEL

CARDBOARD BASE BACKING FOR INSET FRAME

more comfortable for your child's small fingers than your own.) Demonstrate how the knob is actually grasped between the tip of the thumb and the side of the middle finger, while the second finger adds stability and support. See Figure 2. Pick out the insets from their frames. Have your child "feel" the size of the largest rectangle by running her index and middle fingers around its

perimeter. Then ask her to do the same for the corresponding frame. For contrast, she should then feel out the size of the smallest inset and frame. Now, manipulating the inset by its knob, your child may replace the largest rectangle into its frame. Continue in this manner until all the insets are replaced.

Of course, each inset may only fit into one frame. This arrangement presents the idea of order and sequence in terms of size gradation. Your child is already familiar with other kinds of sequences, such as warm-cold, or smooth-rough. Now point out that there is a sequence of pieces from large to small. After a while, you may suggest removing and replacing the insets blindfolded. Holding the inset by its knob with one hand, and feeling out the size of the piece and the frames with the other, your child may enjoy playing the game without looking. Her awareness of the idea of sequence will help her to match the insets and frames correctly.

34

# Chapter 10: Dressing Boards—Part 1

The dressing boards are used in play-exercises designed to teach the skills needed for fastening and unfastening in a variety of ways. Of the seven different boards, the three introduced here are the easiest for younger children to work with: snap board, large-button board, hook-and-eye board. You may ask, why ignore the snowsuit and learn to button or snap on a piece of material tacked to a wooden board? The purpose is to isolate the task in order to develop a skill apart from any complicating factors, such as having to dress in a hurry or cope with tight or loose fitting clothes. Learning the dressing skills independent from the activity of dressing provides for their widest possible application: once your child has learned how to do-up on the dressing board he will have the dexterity to fasten a button, of about the same size, anywhere. The idea of isolating the skill for broader application is an important concept in child development.

MAKING THE DRESSING BOARDS. The dressing board is made simply by tacking a piece of cloth material, outfitted with one kind of fastener, to a small piece of plywood (masonite, pressed wood, or any such sturdy backing). ¼" thickness is sufficient for the backing piece. Cut three 10" x 10" squares. Finish the boards by sanding and shellacking or painting with a neutral color.

Use ³/₁₆" tacks to secure the material to the wood (see Fig. 1). If you do not have access to old garments already equipped with the desired fasteners, you may easily complete the job with some old cloth, a needle and thread. Remember that the cloth pieces will have to be somewhat larger than 10" x 10" to begin with (perhaps 10" x 11"): for they will have to be cut vertically down the middle,

Fig. 1

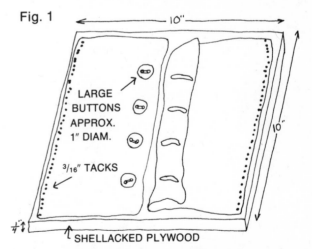

LARGE BUTTONS APPROX. 1" DIAM.

³/₁₆" TACKS

SHELLACKED PLYWOOD

leaving about an inch of material from one side to overlap with the other (see Fig. 2). For the button board, use five or six large buttons (1" diameter). Make sure they are evenly spaced and, of course, evenly lined with the opposite slits. For the snap board—if you cannot find an old pajama top from your child's worn clothes—attach five or six snaps and snap receptacles to the cloth (there is an inexpensive tool made for attaching snaps to material). The snaps should be big enough for a child to manipulate (¼" or ⅜"); but if they are too big, like those on men's jeans, children will have difficulty with them. For the third dressing board, use hooks and eyes of the kind somewhat larger than those usually found on women's dresses.

**BUTTONS**

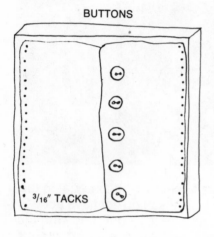

3/16" TACKS

**SNAPS**

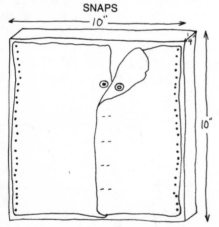

10"

10"

**HOOK & EYE**

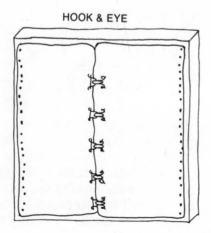

Fig. 2

SNAPPING, BUTTONING, HOOKING. Working at the dressing boards will be great fun for your child. Of the three boards you have made, the hook-and-eye board presents the most problems for younger children. It is best to begin with one of the others. Learning these skills is largely a matter of imitating. While demonstrating, do not crowd over the dressing board. Keep it placed comfortably in front of you, and make sure your child has a good view of all your movements. If you start with the snap board, unfasten each snap separately. Work carefully and slowly. Do not give any impression of tearing open the line of snaps. You may find it worthwhile to practice before demonstrating. Try to analyze the steps you are taking, and become aware of your most significant movements: emphasize those portions of the operation by your actions, without words. Of course, be equally self-conscious and considerate of your child while demonstrating on all the dressing boards. When it is his turn, allow him to experiment alone. If he has problems, you may help by repeating and improving your demonstrations, not by trying to manipulate his fingers with your own. To overcome his difficulties, he should be given a chance to play with the dressing boards for a number of consecutive days.

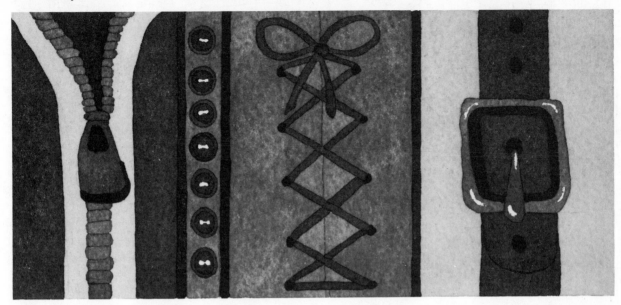

# Chapter 11: Dressing Boards—Part 2

Experience in the classroom has shown that zipping, buckling, lacing, and doing small buttons are more complicated activities for young children than exercising on the first three dressing boards. Yet whatever the difficulties, they always take great joy in overcoming the challenge of one of these boards. Again, with the zipper board, buckle board, lacing board, and small-button board, the tasks are isolated and your child develops her skill by concentrating on a single activity. She does not have to wait for dressing and undressing times to practice with her new jacket: the dressing board is available whenever she wants to play.

MAKING THE BOARDS. The procedure is the same as before. Make four 10″ x 10″ boards with materials tacked on. This time you will need a zipper, some shirt buttons, a long shoe lace, and four buckles (Fig. 1). Be sure that the cloth you choose for each dressing board is suitable to the kind of stress it will receive. The material used with the buckles should be strong enough to withstand the pull needed to buckle-up. For the lacing board, the material must have a double column of holes with ringed reinforcements to prevent tearing from the pull of the lace. One half of the lace itself should be painted, or dyed: the different

colors at each end of the lace will be helpful when it comes to directing the child in the exercise. For the button board, 8 or 10 shirt size buttons (½″ diameter) will be enough. Finally, a zipper should be chosen with your child's fingers in mind.

**Fig. 1** ZIPPER

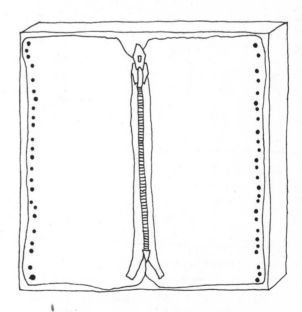

ZIPPING, BUCKLING, BUTTONING, LACING. Approach these exercises as a continuation of the previous three. As success is important for the young child's motivation, the four new tasks should be presented in an order of increasing difficulty: zipper board, buckle board, small-button board, lacing board. But there

BUCKLE

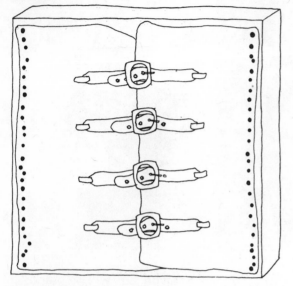

LACE

LACE - HALF-DYED

are quite a few 5 year-olds who cannot do a zipper or who shy away from lacing anything. So if she is not "ready" to work with these dressing boards, make no attempt to

SMALL BUTTONS

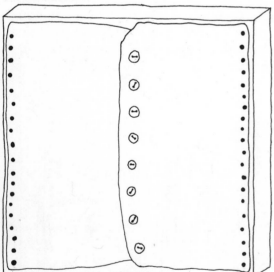

push your child into it. When you do begin to demonstrate, remember to provide your child with as good a view as possible without making the operation awkward for yourself. Be slow, deliberate, and methodical. Try analyzing your own movements in order to convey the essential steps of each fastening and unfastening procedure.

# Chapter 12: Sandpaper Numbers

The concept of number provides the child with his earliest, concrete tool for differentiating entities among all the things around him. **Everything** is broken down into one, or two, or three things: numbers help the child to analyze his environment, to verbalize through symbolic language. The purpose of this chapter is to introduce the child to the shapes and sounds of that language. The fingers play an important part in becoming familiar with each of the number symbols. Your child will learn the forms by "tracing" the sandpaper numbers with his fingers, an action which is basic to the writing exercises that follow. Using sandpaper cut-outs in this play-exercise makes the learning of numbers a combined tactile, visual, and auditory experience.

MAKING THE NUMBERS. All the digits (including zero) can be cut from a single sheet of standard size sandpaper (9″ x 10″). A very fine grade of sandpaper is most appropriate to your child's tactile sensitivity. Using the style of numbers indicated in Figure 1, draw them on the sandpaper with double lines of about ½″ thickness. Each digit should measure about 3½″ high by 2½″ across. Cut out the numbers. Cut a sheet of cardboard (at least 12″ x 12″) into ten pieces measuring 3″ x 4″ each. Glue the sandpaper cut-outs onto the cardboard rectangles (as in Fig. 2).

PLAYING THE NUMBERS. During the play-exercises, your child will become acquainted with the digits by seeing and touching the sandpaper symbols while saying their names. With your index finger and middle finger together, trace over the shape of each number as if you were writing it. Say the name of the number as you move your fingers over it in the direction indicated by the starting-arrows in Figure 3. (or trace the numbers the way you usually write if this

Fig. 1

method does not feel comfortable to you).
Note that the tracing action for digits 4 and 5
requires two separate movements (Fig. 4).

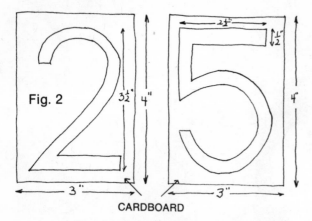

CARDBOARD

Now have your child imitate these actions.
The two-finger tracing movement is the
essence of this exercise. By tracing the
numbers in this way, your child will develop
a heightened sensorial awareness of their
shapes that is not experienced by merely

Fig. 3

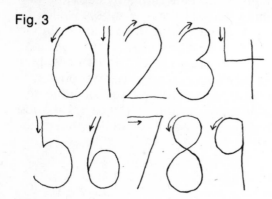

looking at them. He is, of course, also
learning to write. Once adept at these
exercises, he has completed the first phase
of learning numbers. When he has adequate
control of his three writing fingers he is ready
to begin writing the numbers. This activity is
reserved for later exercises.

Fig. 4

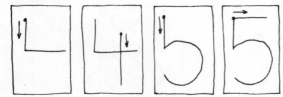

# Chapter 13: Sandpaper Letters

The play-exercise using sandpaper letters is similar to the preceding one. Visual, tactile, and auditory stimuli contribute to teaching the sounds and shapes of letters, the very beginning of reading. Yet, unlike the numbers, there is a crucial distinction that now has to be made between the **names** of the symbols and the **sounds** they convey. Merely to learn the names of the letters, in alphabetical order, is less useful in the learning-to-read process than to understand how the letters function within words, how they sound. It is merely conventional practice which says that a child ought to identify the letters by name **before** learning how they are actually used. Letters, especially the vowels, often stand for more than a single sound. This chapter, by means of the tracing method introduced with the sandpaper numbers, is primarily concerned with presenting the most common phonetic uses of the letters of the alphabet. The letter **a**, therefore, is introduced as it occurs in the word **can**; its sound is suggested by the designation "ah."

MAKING THE LETTERS. To make the letters you will need three or four sheets (9″ x 10″) of very fine grade sandpaper, a sheet of cardboard or posterboard (about 24″ x 36″), and the usual cutting and pasting tools. The style of lettering illustrated in Figure 1 is recommended. If your child's school uses a different style, it would be wise to continue with her accustomed method. In either case, two details are important. (1) Use only lower-case letters; capitals occur relatively infrequently on any page of writing. The child who learns block capitals first will have greater difficulty recognizing

Fig. 1

a e i o u c t s n p g h d
r f l m w y z x v k j b q

41

the symbols that appear on the written or printed page. (2) Letters are different sizes—**a** and **b**, for example—but they must be presented in their proper relative proportions. You should plan your lettering in two sizes: short letters (**a**, **c**, **e**, **n**, **v**, etc.) and tall letters (**b**, **f**, **p**, **t**, etc.). On the sandpaper, draw the short letters approximately 3½" high and 2½" wide (line-thickness about ½"). Make the taller letters approximately 5" x 3". (See Fig. 2.)

**Fig. 2**

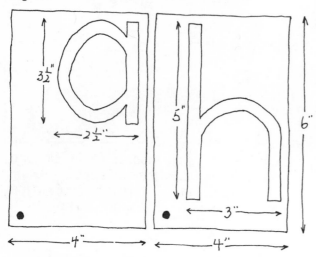

From the sheet (or sheets) of cardboard cut out 26 rectangles, measuring 4" x 6", for backing the letters. Cut out the sandpaper letters, and paste them on the cards, towards the upper right hand corner of the rectangle. Place a red dot at the lower left hand corner of each backing card. The mark indicates where the card should be held, and thus shows the correct orientation for each letter. This is especially important for letters which, like **p** and **d**, if inverted, would become a different letter. (If your child is left-handed, glue the letter towards the upper left hand corner and mark the card on the lower right.)

SOUNDING-OUT THE LETTERS. There is no great advantage in teaching your child the letters alphabetically. In fact, ignoring the alphabetical order may be helpful in some ways. **b** and **d**, because of their similar appearances, may be confusing to the child; they are best presented with a chunk of letters between them. **q** should be saved for the end because of its coupling with -**u**. Moreover, it makes good sense to begin by introducing the five vowels, since these are

encountered more frequently than the other letters, and will appear in all the illustration words.

A handful of letters—**a**, **e**, **i**, **o**, **u**, then—will be more than sufficient for the first day of the exercise. Examine the **Phonetic Chart**. You will be teaching not the letter **e**, but the sound "eh," as in **egg** or **wet**. Teach your child the sounds of the letters by the same method that you used for the names of the numbers. Run your index and middle fingers over the sandpaper letter as if you were writing it. The tracing action should be deliberate and slow. As you do this, say the sound the letter makes, as indicated on the **Phonetic Chart**. Now ask your child to make the tracing movement with her fingers and repeat the sound. Demonstrate how to pronounce the sound with exaggeration, and ask her to do this. Begin with the vowels and proceed down the list with the consonants.

| Phonetic Chart | | | | |
|---|---|---|---|---|
| | a | can, apple | r | run, rat |
| | e | egg, wet | f | fox, fat |
| | i | it, pin | l | lip, leg |
| | o | on, pot | m | mom, mat |
| | u | but, up | w | wet, wax |
| | c | cat, cub | y | yes, yap |
| | t | ten, tub | z | zip, buzz |
| | s | sun, sit | x | box, six |
| | n | nap, net | v | vet, vat |
| | p | pig, pod | k | kit, kettle |
| | g | get, gum | j | jug, jet |
| | h | hat, hug | b | big, bad |
| | d | dot, den | q | quit, quack |

The **Phonetic Chart** illustrates the common sounds with short example words that most children are likely to be familiar with. Of the several sounds possibly designated by some letters in the English alphabet, the one which occurs most frequently in the child's vocabulary is illustrated here for teaching purposes. Once the individual phonemes are learned, an entire word can be comprehended as a phonetic unit. But perhaps this is jumping the gun a bit. Phonetic pronunciation of whole words is a subject covered in a different part of this book. At this point it is sufficient that your child be aware of the main sound represented by each sandpaper symbol. Learning these letters through the tracing and pronouncing method will undoubtedly be a long-term project. Perhaps just a few letters a day, with periodic review exercises, would be the best way to proceed.

# Chapter 14: Basic Writing

This chapter is a natural extension of the exercises involving the sandpaper numbers and letters. Once your child has become familiar with their names, sounds, and shapes, he will be eager to reproduce the letters and digits with a pencil on his own. The importance of the three-finger dexterity is now most obvious. Proper manipulation of the writing implement will naturally give the best results. Beyond the neurological factor of hand-and-eye coordination, learning to write is largely a matter of practice and repetition. The writing sheets in the following play-exercises are designed to accomodate to the need for such repetitive practice. Writing the same letters and numbers over and over again might seem tedious to an adult, but to a little person the process is indeed valuable child's work.

PREPARING THE MATERIALS. All the materials are provided in this book: the three letter-sheets and one number-sheet. Your child may write directly on the pages that follow. But surely you will want to have additional copies of these writing sheets. Ideally, it would be best to photocopy several of each of the sheets before your child makes his initial marks on them. If a photocopy machine is not available to you, or if you would rather avoid the expense, simply make extra pages on 8½" x 11" paper with a pencil and ruler as the need arises.

Note that each letter-sheet measures 7" x 9", thus containing 63 one-inch squares. The number-sheet contains 10 rows, making 70 squares in all. The one-inch square is a convenient space for your child to begin writing in. Leave a space for the date at the bottom of each writing-sheet to keep a record of your child's progress.

WRITING. The letters are presented in an order generally representing their frequency of occurrence or usefulness for the child. Of course your child might have a special interest in some particular letters that do not come at the beginning; you should not discourage him from working early with any letter from the latter parts of the sheets. But the first letter-sheet will probably prove to be of greatest value to the beginner.

Working with the writing-sheets involves three stages. First, with his pencil, your child should trace over the letter (or number) as it appears in the left-hand column of the writing-sheet. Second, he should again make the same letter or number by completing the dotted outlines in the next two columns of the same row. Finally, he may practice the writing on his own in the remaining empty squares. Use this procedure for practicing with all the numbers and letters. Note the position of the figures within the squares. Many of them, like a, c, s, m, v, fall within the center of each square. Some, however, extend down to the base-line (for example, p, g, j, y), while others reach up to the top (d, f, h, k, l). Your child should be reminded of the relative sizes of these letters, and of the relationship between letter and line, as he practices with each figure.

As your child is working at these play-exercises, you should bear in mind the following helpful hints:

1. Make sure your child is always holding the pencil in the proper three-fingered way.

2. Encourage him to complete one whole page at a time. Children get more satisfaction from completed work.

3. When your child first traces over a letter (or number) with his pencil, ask him to say its sound (or name).

4. If he shows a preference for his left hand, do not discourage him from using it.

5. Encourage your child to practice his writing even if at times he seems reluctant. Becoming involved and completing the work with your encouragement will provide the satisfaction that he needs to keep at it.

6. If he is writing poorly, try not to say, "That's wrong!" Rather, point out the best written letter in a row of, say, t's, and tell him, "this is the best t—try to make another just like it."

7. For you and your child alike, remember: being involved with the letters and numbers is most important; accuracy comes with practice.

| a | a | a | | | | |
|---|---|---|---|---|---|---|
| e | e | e | | | | |
| i | i | i | | | | |
| o | o | o | | | | |
| u | u | u | | | | |
| c | c | c | | | | |
| t | t | t | | | | |
| s | s | s | | | | |
| n | n | n | | | | |

date _____

| | | | | | | |
|---|---|---|---|---|---|---|
| p | p | p | | | | |
| g | g | g | | | | |
| h | h | h | | | | |
| d | d | d | | | | |
| r | r | r | | | | |
| f | f | f | | | | |
| l | l | l | | | | |
| m | m | m | | | | |
| w | w | w | | | | |

date _____

Letter-Sheet: 3

| | | | | | | |
|---|---|---|---|---|---|---|
| y | y | y | | | | |
| z | z | z | | | | |
| x | x | x | | | | |
| v | v | v | | | | |
| k | k | k | | | | |
| j | j | j | | | | |
| b | b | b | | | | |
| q | q | q | | | | |

date _____

Number-Sheet

| | | | | | | |
|---|---|---|---|---|---|---|
| 0 | 0 | 0 | | | | |
| 1 | 1 | 1 | | | | |
| 2 | 2 | 2 | | | | |
| 3 | 3 | 3 | | | | |
| 4 | 4 | 4 | | | | |
| 5 | 5 | 5 | | | | |
| 6 | 6 | 6 | | | | |
| 7 | 7 | 7 | | | | |
| 8 | 8 | 8 | | | | |
| 9 | 9 | 9 | | | | |

date _____

| | | | | | | |
|---|---|---|---|---|---|---|
| a | a | a | | | | |
| e | e | e | | | | |
| i | i | i | | | | |
| o | o | o | | | | |
| u | u | u | | | | |
| c | c | c | | | | |
| t | t | t | | | | |
| s | s | s | | | | |
| n | n | n | | | | |

date _____

| p | p | p | | | | |
| g | g | g | | | | |
| h | h | h | | | | |
| d | d | d | | | | |
| r | r | r | | | | |
| f | f | f | | | | |
| l | l | l | | | | |
| m | m | m | | | | |
| W | w | w | | | | |

date _____

| | | | | | | |
|---|---|---|---|---|---|---|
| y | y | y | | | | |
| z | z | z | | | | |
| x | x | x | | | | |
| v | v | v | | | | |
| k | k | k | | | | |
| j | j | j | | | | |
| b | b | b | | | | |
| q | q | q | | | | |

date _____

Number-Sheet *(extra)*

| 0 | 0 | 0 | | | | |
|---|---|---|---|---|---|---|
| 1 | 1 | 1 | | | | |
| 2 | 2 | 2 | | | | |
| 3 | 3 | 3 | | | | |
| 4 | 4 | 4 | | | | |
| 5 | 5 | 5 | | | | |
| 6 | 6 | 6 | | | | |
| 7 | 7 | 7 | | | | |
| 8 | 8 | 8 | | | | |
| 9 | 9 | 9 | | | | |

date _____

# Part III: Size, Shape & Form

Working with geometric toys can be among the most stimulating and compelling activities for young children. The games in the next four chapters familiarize your child with basic geometric designs, while building upon some of the ideas and methods introduced in the earlier play-exercises. But each one of the activities involving size, shape or form can be approached freshly and apart from the previous context.

# Chapter 15: Sequence Boxes

The arrangement of ordered sequences has come up in connection with several of the play-exercises from Parts I and II. So far, your child has worked with sequences of sound pitch, color shading, weight and temperature, fabric texture, and rectangular size. In most of those exercises, observing sequences was secondary to a larger concern. In this chapter, the concept of sequence itself is the main subject to be explored. In particular, your child will be working with size-gradation of boxes and objects that fit in them. The sequence boxes are five cardboard boxes of varying size that are made to accomodate different objects, also graded, in a fixed order. Thus your child will actually be working with the relationships between two sequences, and during the play-exercises she will learn to perceive both harmony and disproportion between the objects and the boxes.

BUILDING THE BOXES. Because special sizes are required for these exercises, one of your main roles in the sequence games involves making the boxes and their lids to prescribed dimensions. Several sheets of cardboard—five different colors of posterboard, preferably—will be needed for the construction. Also needed are a ruler, scissors, a razor knife, pencil, and some adhesive tape. All the boxes are square,

varying in size by increments of ½″; the height of the sides is the same for each, 1½″. For the sake of an easy, overlapping fit, the lids are made slightly larger than their boxes. The **Table of Dimensions** summarizes the essential information in the following description.

| Table of Dimensions | | | |
|---|---|---|---|
| Box: | Base | Height | Lid |
| largest 1 | 4″ sq. x | 1½″ | 4⅛″ sq. x ½″ |
| 2 | 3½″ sq. x | 1½″ | 3⅝″ sq. x ½″ |
| 3 | 3″ sq. x | 1½″ | 3⅛″ sq. x ½″ |
| 4 | 2½″ sq. x | 1½″ | 2⅝″ sq. x ½″ |
| smallest 5 | 2″ sq. x | 1½″ | 2⅛″ sq. x ½″ |

To make the first and largest box, having a base 4″ square, draw and then cut a square measuring 7″ x 7″ on the first piece of cardboard. From each corner of the seven-inch square, cut out a 1½″ square. The resulting shape (see Fig. 1) prepares you to fold up the 1½″ sides around the 4″ square base; with a pencil and a straightedge, this basic square should now be indicated by dotted lines.

The remaining four boxes are drafted in parallel fashion. For the second box, with a base 3½″ square, outline and cut a 6½″ square on the cardboard. Then, as above, cut out 1½″ squares from each of the corners

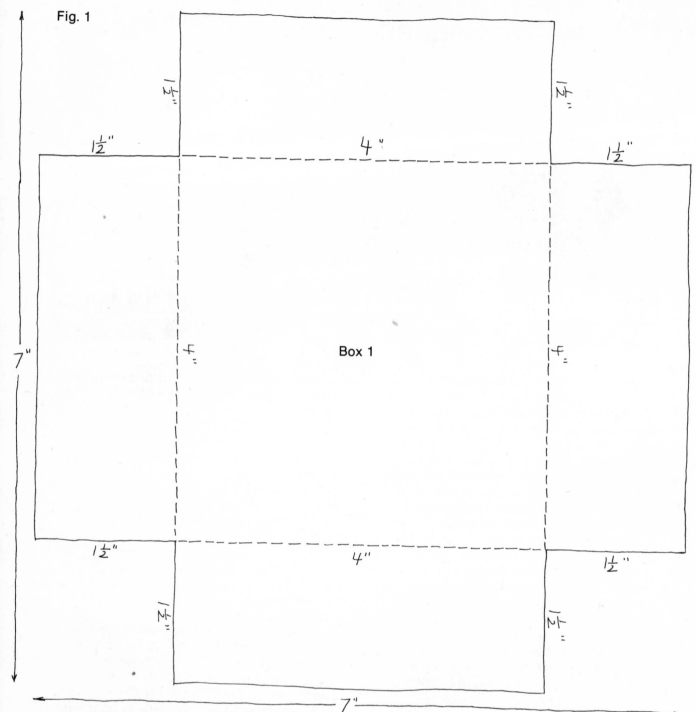

Fig. 1

$1\frac{1}{2}''$

$1\frac{1}{2}''$

$1\frac{1}{2}''$   4 "   $1\frac{1}{2}''$

7 "

4 "   Box 1   4 "

$1\frac{1}{2}''$   4"   $1\frac{1}{2}''$

$1\frac{1}{2}''$   $1\frac{1}{2}''$

7"

(Fig. 2). Draft the next three boxes by measuring squares 6″, 5½″, and 5″; remove the 1½″ corners from each of these (Fig. 3).

Preparation of the lids, which overlap the sides of the boxes by ½″, involves the same process described above. Only the measurements differ. The square tops of the lids measure ⅛″ larger than their corresponding boxes. Thus the lids are

drafted on the cardboard as squares measuring 5⅛″, 4⅝″, 4⅛″, 3⅝″, and 3⅛″. Now, ½″ squares are cut from the corners of each of these five squares (see Fig. 4). As with the boxes, a pencil guided by a straightedge should be used to indicate the lines along which the folding of the sides will be made.

The ten pieces are now ready to be folded

64

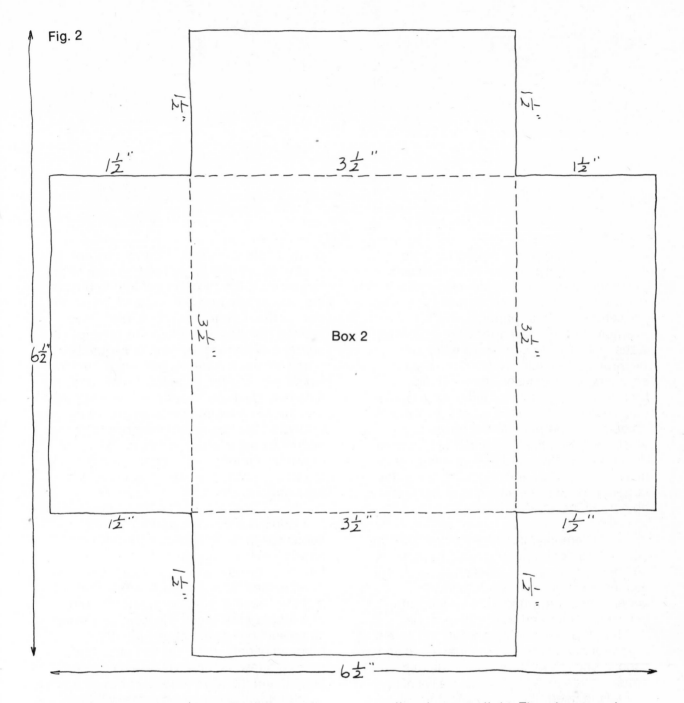

Fig. 2

$1\frac{1}{2}$"

$1\frac{1}{2}$"

$1\frac{1}{2}$"    $3\frac{1}{2}$"    $1\frac{1}{2}$"

$3\frac{1}{4}$"    Box 2    $3\frac{1}{2}$"

$6\frac{1}{2}$"

$1\frac{1}{2}$"    $3\frac{1}{2}$"    $1\frac{1}{2}$"

$1\frac{1}{2}$"

$1\frac{1}{2}$"

$6\frac{1}{2}$"

and taped into finished form. To make each folding accurate, with a razor knife lightly score the surface along the pencilled outline of the square. Bend the cardboard and fold up the four sides. Carefully tape the joining edges, both inside and out, on each of the boxes and lids (see Fig. 5).

WORKING WITH SEQUENCE SETS. For the purpose of this chapter, a sequence set is defined as a series of similar objects that shows a quantitative gradation, from large to

small, or heavy to light. The play-exercises consist mainly of correctly placing sequence sets of various objects in the sequence boxes. Objects that may be used for sequence sets are easy to find in the household. Five different sized nails arranged from long to short provide a good example of "length sequence." Five bolts of the same length but of different diameter show "weight sequence." Five different sized buttons—clothing buttons, campaign buttons, smile buttons—may be put into the

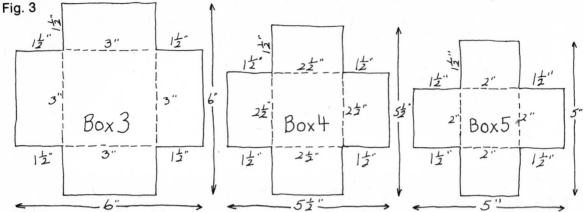

Fig. 3

Box 3 — $1\frac{1}{2}''$, $3''$, $1\frac{1}{2}''$; $3''$, $3''$; $6''$; $1\frac{1}{2}''$, $3''$, $1\frac{1}{2}''$; $6''$

Box 4 — $1\frac{1}{2}''$, $2\frac{1}{2}''$, $1\frac{1}{2}''$; $2\frac{1}{2}''$, $2\frac{1}{2}''$; $5\frac{1}{2}''$; $1\frac{1}{2}''$, $2\frac{1}{2}''$, $1\frac{1}{2}''$; $5\frac{1}{2}''$

Box 5 — $1\frac{1}{2}''$, $2''$, $1\frac{1}{2}''$; $2''$, $2''$; $5''$; $1\frac{1}{2}''$, $2''$, $1\frac{1}{2}''$; $5''$

boxes to illustrate size sequence. Five different sizes of plant leaves, or five sizes of plastic farm or zoo animals, also make a good sequence set. You can make your own sequence sets with paper cut-outs. For example, cut out of a magazine five different sizes of a favorite number or letter; or pictures of thematically related objects showing size-gradation (for example, transportation theme: a jumbo jet, a bus, a car, a bicycle, and roller skates). All of these objects may be put into the boxes to illustrate sequence. The important point to remember is always to keep the largest or heaviest object of any sequence set in the largest box, and the smallest or lightest objects in the smallest box.

As you demonstrate with the boxes and the objects, be deliberate with your movements and precise in your explanation of the idea of sequence. Make sure your child understands the proportional relationship between object and box. You must be mindful of proportion, too, when you select your sequence sets. The number set, if you choose one, should consist of cut-outs proportionate to the box sizes. If a set of toy animals is used, its pieces should be proportionate to their relative life sizes: do not use a toy chicken larger than a toy bull. The transportation picture cut-outs should be made to fit unfolded in each box.

For the initial play-exercises, one or two sequence sets ought to be sufficient. With one or two sets placed in the lidded boxes, begin by showing your child the arrangement of boxes from large to small. Then remove the objects of one sequence set from the boxes and show her how each is

graded next to its box. That is, explain, for example, that the largest leaf is next to the largest box; the next largest leaf is beside the next largest box; the middle sized leaf is next to the middle sized box; etc. This method teaches your child the principle of verbal comparison as well as sequential order. When illustrating sequence, use the words big, bigger, biggest, small, smaller, smallest. Next, point out how each leaf fits into its own special empty box. Now try arranging the boxes and the objects of one sequence set in a random order. Your child may then attempt to rearrange the objects in the boxes in their proper sequential order from large to small.

A good exercise illustrating length sequence is done by cutting a few plastic straws into five lengths of (1) five inches, (2) four and one half inches, (3) four inches, (4) three inches, and (5) two and one half inches. These should be cut neatly and placed diagonally in the boxes: the largest straw section—five inches—will fit diagonally only in the largest box. The second straw section will fit only in the largest and the second largest boxes. Each of the remaining three sections will fit diagonally in all of the boxes larger than its own length, but not in those boxes which are smaller. Error becomes apparent in a straw exercise when one section is out of place, causing another not to fit in the remaining box. You may think of many games and variations to play with the five boxes and the sequence sets. Making a new sequence set every once in a while will keep your child interested. Once she has become familiar with the idea of sequence, the boxes may be used merely for storing the toys.

66

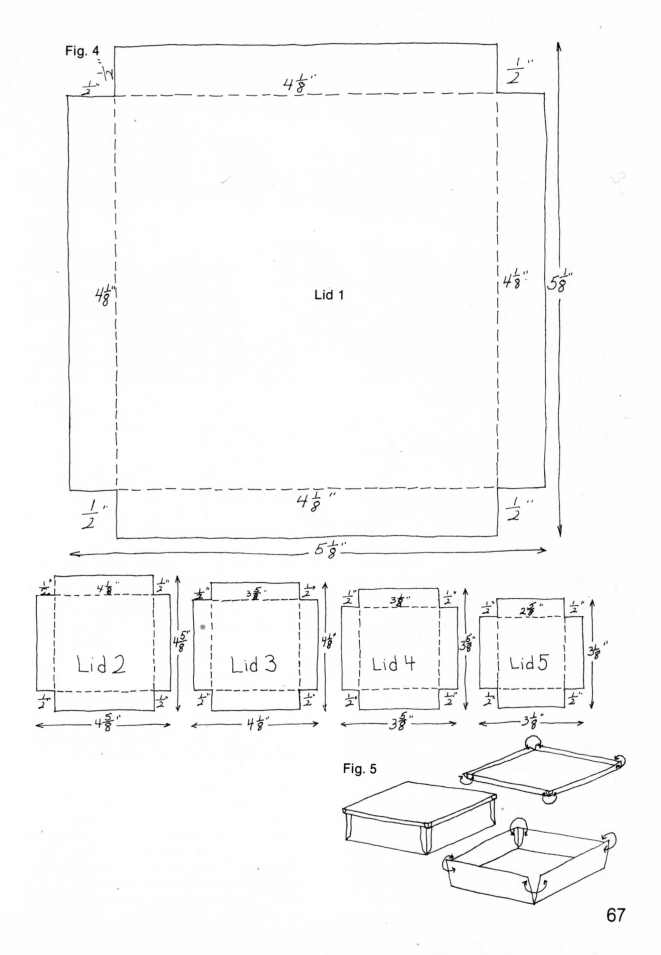

Fig. 4

$\frac{1}{2}$"

$\frac{1}{2}$"

$4\frac{1}{8}$"

$\frac{1}{2}$"

$4\frac{1}{8}$"

Lid 1

$4\frac{1}{8}$"

$5\frac{1}{8}$"

$\frac{1}{2}$"

$4\frac{1}{8}$"

$\frac{1}{2}$"

$5\frac{1}{8}$"

$\frac{1}{2}$"

$4\frac{1}{8}$"

$\frac{1}{2}$"

Lid 2

$\frac{1}{2}$"

$\frac{1}{2}$"

$4\frac{5}{8}$"

$4\frac{5}{8}$"

$\frac{1}{2}$"

$3\frac{5}{8}$"

$\frac{1}{2}$"

Lid 3

$\frac{1}{2}$"

$\frac{1}{2}$"

$4\frac{1}{8}$"

$4\frac{1}{8}$"

$\frac{1}{2}$"

$3\frac{1}{8}$"

$\frac{1}{2}$"

Lid 4

$\frac{1}{2}$"

$\frac{1}{2}$"

$3\frac{5}{8}$"

$3\frac{5}{8}$"

$\frac{1}{2}$"

$2\frac{5}{8}$"

$\frac{1}{2}$"

Lid 5

$\frac{1}{2}$"

$\frac{1}{2}$"

$3\frac{1}{8}$"

$3\frac{1}{8}$"

Fig. 5

67

# Chapter 16: Geometric Frames and Insets

Toys that teach the common geometric shapes are among the most popular commercially available games for young children. Often they are manufactured from fine, hard woods, brightly and variously painted, and not inexpensive. Exercising a bit of your own creative ingenuity, you can (with considerably less expense and more personal reward) make an equally functional and attractive set of geometric shapes for your child to work with. Moreover, you can add to these a number of designs and shapes that are not commonly found in the store-bought products. Irregular geometric shapes, for example, or animals, houses, cars, leaf shapes, etc., might be of interest to your child. Any small magazine photo can be traced onto cardboard and used for an inset. These, in addition to the geometric shapes described below, will provide further enjoyment for your child's frame and inset game. As in many of the play-exercises presented in this book, the dexterity factor is a key to success. The toy in this chapter exercises the three-finger sense in a game that stresses recognition and manipulation of plane geometric forms. In addition, the frames and insets are used as guidelines for drawing forms with a pencil.

MAKING THE INSETS AND FRAMES. The insets are made by cutting geometric designs out of cardboard squares, leaving frames in which the shapes can be replaced (Fig. 1). To make a good set of shapes and frames you will need some sturdy cardboard (about two square feet), a 6″ piece of wooden dowel (about ⅜″ in diameter), strong glue, two colors of paint, scissors, razor knife, ruler, compass, and protractor. Eight geometric insets are described here, though you may, now or at a later time, wish to add some of the other forms suggested above. The insets can be made in the following steps:

(1) Cut out eight cardboard squares, measuring 6″ x 6″.

(2) Locate the center point of each by intersecting two diagonals (Fig. 2). The center mark represents the point of attachment for the pick-up knobs.

(3) Draw the geometric figure, centered in the square. With a protractor, ruler, and compass, plan your designs according to the measurements indicated in Figure 1. Each figure (except the trapezoid) should be

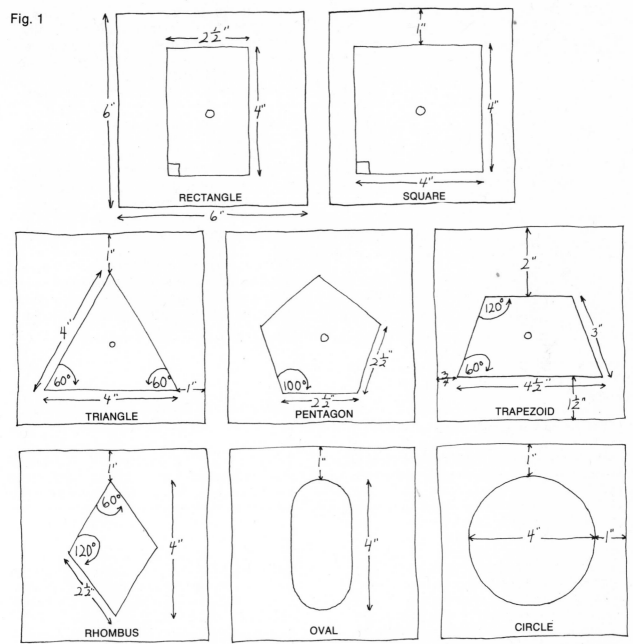

Fig. 1

RECTANGLE

SQUARE

TRIANGLE

PENTAGON

TRAPEZOID

RHOMBUS

OVAL

CIRCLE

drawn with a margin at all points of about ¾"-1" to the outer edge of the square (Fig. 2). Note that an oval is made by drawing a pair of 2"-diameter circles tangent to one another (Fig. 3).

(4) Making firm, deep slices into the cardboard, use a razor knife to cut out the shapes with precision.

(5) Make pick-up knobs for each inset with a piece of wooden dowel cut to ½". Glue the sanded knob over the diagonal intersection at the center of each inset.

(6) Paint all the insets one color and all the frames another. Painting will add rigidity to the cardboard while covering the sketch lines and making all the pieces more attractive.

HANDLING THE INSETS AND DRAWING THE SHAPES. Both parts of the play-exercise will acquaint your child with geometric shapes while developing his three-finger sense. Picking up the insets properly, with three fingers around the knob, is good practice for writing. Indeed, furthering the child's facility with the

**Fig. 2**

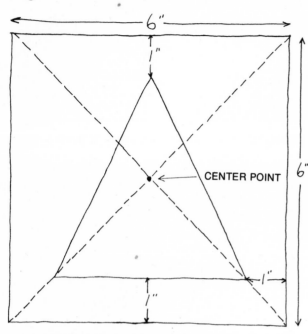

6"

CENTER POINT

6"

may want to replace the inset by sliding it across the frame: demonstrate how easily and precisely the inset can be maneuvered by twisting the knob. Note that most of the shapes can be set in their frames in a number of ways. Rotate the knobs in order to test these insets for all possible fitting positions. If accurately cut, the pentagon, square, and triangle should each fit into its frame in five, four, and three ways, respectively. The rectangle, rhombus, and oval should each fit in two ways. Teach your child the names of the geometric shapes by the three-point method suggested earlier for the color cards.

When your child is familiar with the shapes and their names, he is ready to use the insets and frames for tracing geometric designs on paper. Be sure that he holds the pencil in the

**Fig. 3**

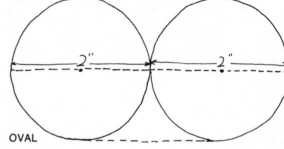

2"          2"

OVAL

mechanics of pencil manipulation is one of the most significant aspects of these activities.

The primary exercise involves removing the insets from their frames and replacing them. Show your child how to lift the inset by manipulating its knob with three fingers. He

**Fig. 4**

70

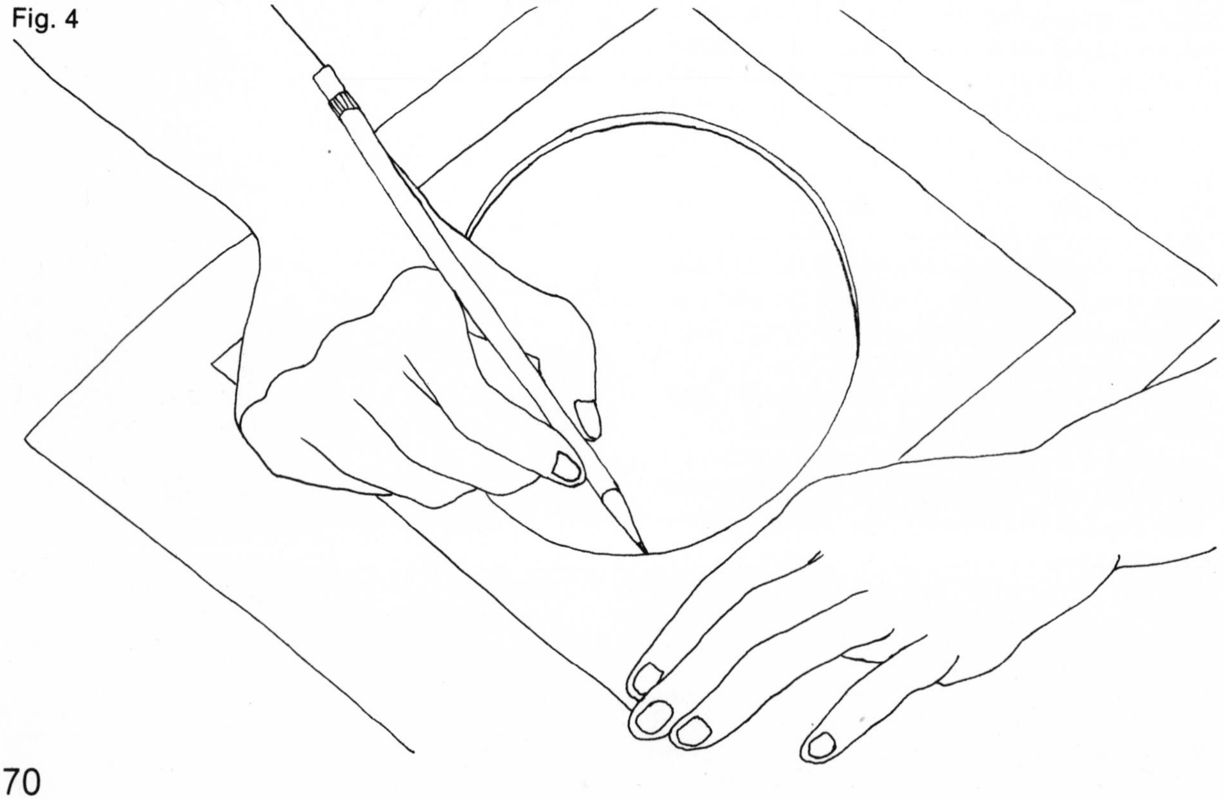

**Fig. 5**

CIRCLE FRAME &
WITH INSET PARALLEL LINES

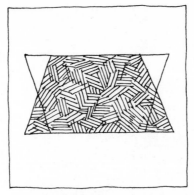

TRAPEZOID FRAME & UPSIDE DOWN

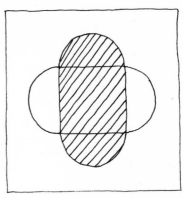

OVAL & TURNED 90°

SQUARE & RHOMBUS

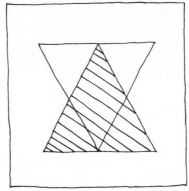

TRIANGLE FRAME & UPSIDE DOWN

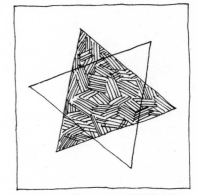

TRIANGLE INSET TURNED 45°

three-fingered way. For most children, tracing around the inner part of a frame seems easier than tracing around the edge of an inset. Begin, then, by tracing the inner circumference of the circle frame. Show your child how to steady the frame with his free hand while completing the circle without lifting his pencil off the paper (Fig. 4). Now let him attempt to draw the same shape by tracing around the outer edge of the circular inset. The same method should be used for drawing the other geometric shapes. You may wish to point out that the two circular tracings—one made with the inset and one with the frame—can be combined to produce a double circle. Figure 5 shows a variety of exciting forms that your child can draw by superimposing one outline upon another.

# Chapter 17: Construction Triangles

The game in this chapter involves sensorial work with form. Using a variety of triangular forms, children can channel their inherent creativity into the making of exciting geometric shapes. The simple construction triangles can be combined and arranged to form complicated patterns of basic artistic design. By making new forms from familiar ones, your child will expand her imaginative range, while at the same time exercising her hand-and-eye coordination and three-finger dexterity. Working with the construction triangles will appeal to a wide span of age groups. Younger children (from about 2½ years and up) will be attracted to the simplicity of the basic shapes, while the older ones (6-to-65) will be intrigued by the potentially complex arrangements of these forms.

MAKING THE TRIANGLES. The triangles are simply made by drawing the patterns on thick cardboard with a pencil, protractor, and ruler, and cutting them out with a scissors or razor knife. (If you are handy with a saw, you may choose to make a more durable set of triangles out of ¼" plywood, masonite, or linoleum tile.) Four different kinds of triangles are needed. These are illustrated in Figure 1 in their actual sizes. You may either trace these onto your material, or copy them according to the angles and dimensions indicated.

Triangle A: right-angled isosceles (two equal sides, two equal angles, plus right-angle). Make 4 of these.

Triangle B: isosceles (two equal sides, two equal angles). Make 6 of these.

Triangle C: equilateral (three equal sides, three equal angles) Make 6.

Triangle D: right-angled (three different sides, three different angles, including right-angle). Make 4.

There are 20 triangles in all. As you can see, the sides of some of the triangles are equal in length to the sides of some others. These equal lengths, which represent the joining edges in the formation of new shapes, are indicated in Figure 1 by the small letters a and b. Only two lengths—side d from Triangle A and side c from Triangle D—have no equal counterparts in the other triangles. Keep all the pieces in a shoebox, referred to as the "triangle box." If you decide to paint this set of toys, make the triangles either all one color, or a different color for each of the four kinds.

CREATING NEW FORMS. The twenty triangles can be arranged in groups to make six rectangles. Figure 2 illustrates this arrangement. The triangles thus combined

Fig. 1

ACTUAL SIZE

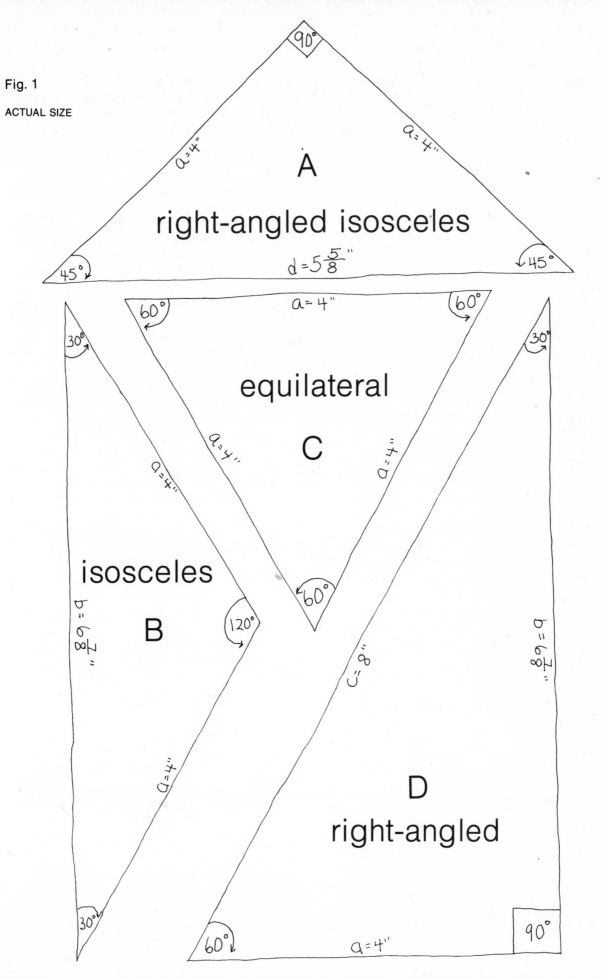

A

right-angled isosceles

equilateral

C

isosceles

B

D

right-angled

**Fig. 2** PACKING GROUPS OF TRIANGLES

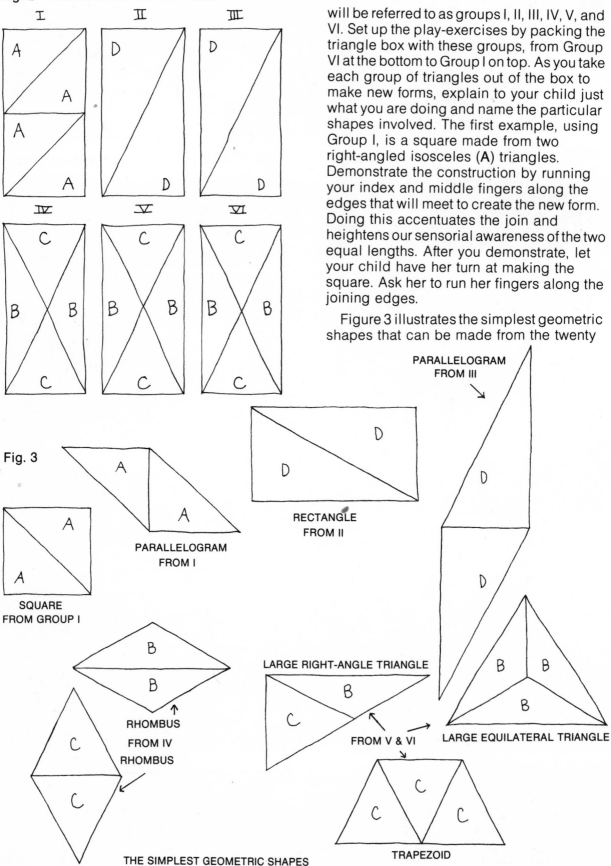

will be referred to as groups I, II, III, IV, V, and VI. Set up the play-exercises by packing the triangle box with these groups, from Group VI at the bottom to Group I on top. As you take each group of triangles out of the box to make new forms, explain to your child just what you are doing and name the particular shapes involved. The first example, using Group I, is a square made from two right-angled isosceles (**A**) triangles. Demonstrate the construction by running your index and middle fingers along the edges that will meet to create the new form. Doing this accentuates the join and heightens our sensorial awareness of the two equal lengths. After you demonstrate, let your child have her turn at making the square. Ask her to run her fingers along the joining edges.

Figure 3 illustrates the simplest geometric shapes that can be made from the twenty

**Fig. 3**

SQUARE
FROM GROUP I

PARALLELOGRAM
FROM I

RECTANGLE
FROM II

PARALLELOGRAM
FROM III

LARGE EQUILATERAL TRIANGLE

RHOMBUS
FROM IV
RHOMBUS

LARGE RIGHT-ANGLE TRIANGLE

FROM V & VI

THE SIMPLEST GEOMETRIC SHAPES

TRAPEZOID

Fig. 4

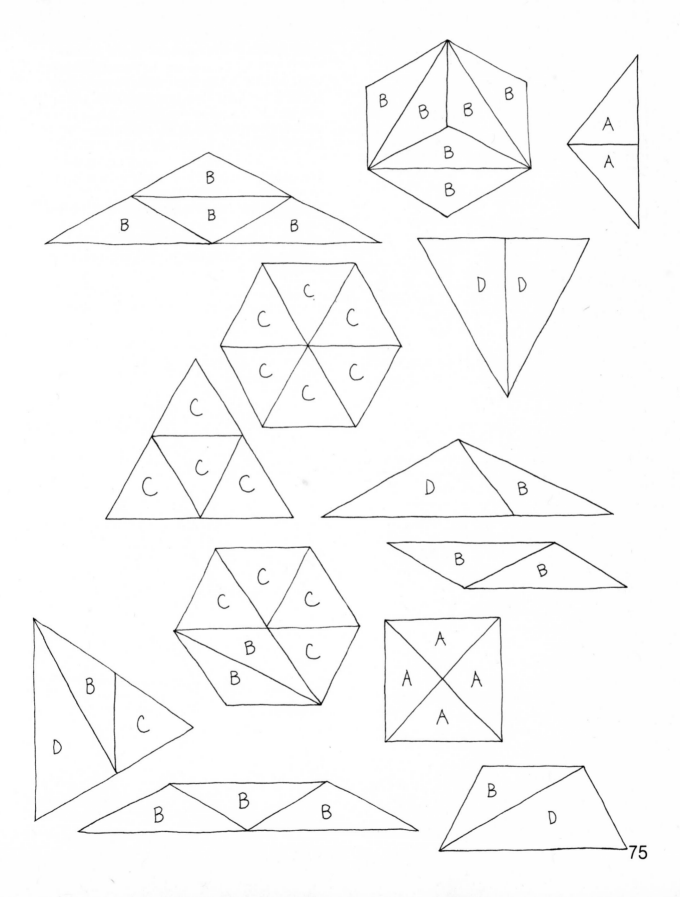

triangles as you bring them out, one group at a time, from the triangle box. From Group I you can demonstrate a square and parallelogram made of two pieces each. Leave these on display and bring out Groups II and III. These can be used to illustrate a rectangle and another, more elongated, parallelogram. Group IV—comprising two equilateral and two isosceles triangles—can be rearranged into two different forms of a rhombus. The eight triangles of Groups V and VI illustrate the construction of new and familiar shapes. Explain to your child, and demonstrate how three equilateral triangles (C) may form a trapezoid. A large equilateral triangle can be constructed from three smaller isosceles triangles (B). The two triangles now remaining from Groups V and VI—one equilateral and one isosceles—may be joined to make a large, right-angled triangle, the same size as one of the original D triangles. Using all twenty triangles, you now have on display nine basic geometric forms. After your child has experimented with each of them, replace them in the box according to the original groups.

Have your child remove the pieces from the triangle box and do some constructing on her own. Do not hesitate to tell her the proper geometric terms. Teach the names of the different triangles and the new forms by the three-step method. With two or three shapes displayed at a time, say, for example, (1) this is an equilateral triangle; (2) show me the equilateral triangle; (3) which one is this? (pointing to the equilateral triangle). There is a multitude of different forms that these triangles can construct. Figure 4 indicates only a few. Encourage your child to experiment and create new forms. Remind her, when she is finished playing, to replace the pieces orderly in the triangle box. Making these six groups of rectangles is always the last step in the game.

# Part IV: Numbers

For children as well as adults, working with numbers can be as exciting as it is challenging. The key to success lies in the manner of presentation. In these chapters, the language of numbers is made entirely realistic through the concrete representation of actual quantities. A variety of stimulating toys will invite your child to enjoy the working out of simple mathematical relationships and exercises.

# Chapter 18: Geometric Solids

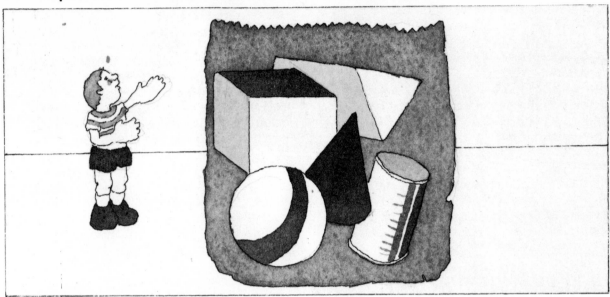

At a young age children develop the ability to identify objects solely through the sense of touch. Perceiving the material qualities of an object—its form and weight—leads to a recognition of the object itself. (Such perception is known as the stereognostic sense.) We experience this kind of recognition when, for example, we reach into a pocket of loose change and correctly identify a dime. In this chapter, the sense of tactile recognition will be stimulated by geometric solids. Your child will not only cultivate the sensorial experience, but simultaneously will learn to identify the most common solid geometric shapes.

PROVIDING THE SOLIDS. The solid geometric forms to be used in the following play-exercises are indicated in Figure 1. You should have no trouble finding examples of most of these around your household. Many sets of children's blocks—the large wooden ones, or the small, interlocking, plastic pieces—will furnish examples of all, except for the sphere. The sphere, however, is simple enough to present in the form of a rubber ball, an orange, etc. A cylinder may be illustrated by a small, aluminum juice can (empty the juice, if you wish, through small pin holes). A rectangular prism is exemplified in a cigarette box, taped closed, or any small gift box. A conical paper cup, or

Fig. 1

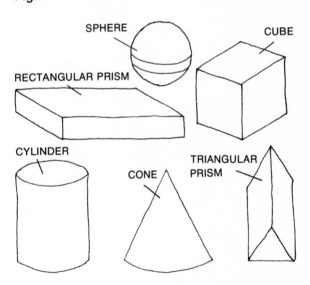

SPHERE    CUBE
RECTANGULAR PRISM
CYLINDER    CONE    TRIANGULAR PRISM

a party hat, for example, illustrates the cone shape. Look around your child's toy chest, your kitchen cupboard or junk drawer for examples of such objects. A trip to the supermarket ought to reveal some usable, variously shaped containers that might normally escape your notice. It is advisable to paint whatever cardboard boxes or containers you choose; this will make them more sturdy while highlighting the shapes and properly de-emphasizing any irrelevant particulars on the containers themselves. Also, try to procure relatively small objects—a juice can is a better cylinder than an oatmeal container—since all are going to be placed in a single bag for identification during the exercises.

Should you prefer to construct some of the shapes out of cardboard, follow the blueprints in Figure 2 for the cube, triangular prism, and rectangular prism. Simple cutting, folding, and taping operations, as suggested in the diagrams, will produce the sturdy solids. Because of their curvatures, the cone, cylinder, and sphere present some construction problems that may best be avoided by procuring the already-formed objects. Obtain either a blindfold or a non-transparent bag large enough to contain all the objects you decide to use.

IDENTIFYING THE SHAPES. Begin these play-exercises by teaching your child the names of these geometric solids. In addition

to the objects themselves, you may show him the pictures in Figure 1. When presenting a rubber ball, for example, be sure to emphasize that you are teaching the name of the **shape**, not the object. Otherwise you might give your child the sphere and hear him reply, "no daddy that is not a sphere that is a rubber ball." Have him compare the sphere with, say, the rectangular prism. Point out that the latter is flat, sharp-angled, has corners, six sides, and looks different from different angles. The sphere is round, has really only one surface, and looks and feels the same from any angle. Continue to name all the solids and compare them in such ways with one another. For your child, **feeling** the shapes of these forms is the most important facet of the game.

When he is comfortable with three or four of them, put these solids into a large bag. Ask him to feel around with both hands

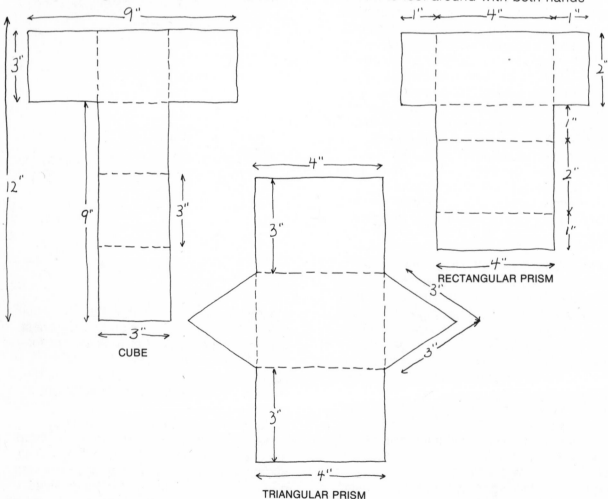

CUBE

TRIANGULAR PRISM

RECTANGULAR PRISM

Fig. 2

inside the bag and identify the objects one at a time. Then he may bring out the object for a visual check. Discovering the shapes inside the bag will be an exciting experience for children, and even more challenging as the number of objects is increased. Once he has learned to identify all the geometric shapes, it will be fun to put different kinds of objects in with them, creating a "mystery bag."

First, let him see the new objects that you put in the bag—almost anything will do: a coin, a banana, a chapstick, a small book, a light bulb, a jelly bean. Now ask him to reach in and identify these objects by their feel. Perhaps he will be able to perceive a kind of similarity between the shapes of the geometric solids and these new objects. Let him discover, for example, that a banana is slightly cylindrical, a jelly bean nearly spherical, the book rectangular, etc. To vary the game, you might later secretly introduce some more common objects and ask your child to try to name by feeling everything in the mystery bag.

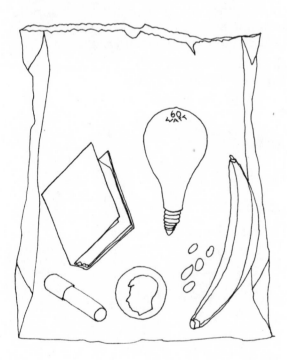

# Chapter 19: Number Box

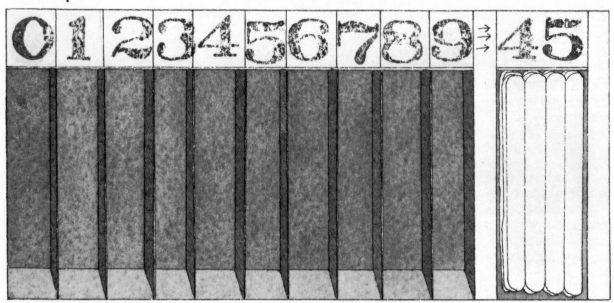

Children learn to count to ten before comprehending the numerical value of each digit. The number box tangibly demonstrates these values by making the association between the number symbol itself and the quantity of items designated by that symbol. Using the number box, moreover, enables the child not only to observe, but to experience actively the meaning of quantity. The play-exercise also introduces the concept of zero as both the idea of nothing and a part of the numbered progression to ten. For your child, working with the number box will be a joyful game.

MAKING THE NUMBER BOX. 45 ice-cream sticks (sold in most supermarkets), or 45 wooden dowels, pencils, etc., will be used with the box itself. You will also need some strong cardboard, paint, tape, glue, scissors, and a razor knife. Almost any sturdy cardboard box will do—a shoebox, a large stationery box, etc. Two cigar boxes, taped together or not, would be ideal for size and sturdiness. The box should be without a top, but have a rigid back that extends higher than the sides (see Fig. 1). Cut to proper size and glue a piece of rigid cardboard to the back of the box. (If you have two cigar boxes, you may slit off their lids to use as the backing pieces.) Section the box (or boxes) into ten (or five) parts of equal size by taping in rectangular dividers, cut accurately out of the strong cardboard (Fig. 1). Be careful to ensure that the width of each numbered section is identical. You may want to paint the fully constructed number box with any neutral color. Use a felt-tip pen to indicate the numbered divisions.

Fig. 1

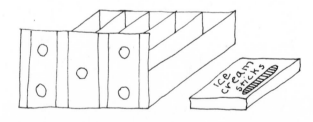

TAPE  WHERE 4 EDGES MEET

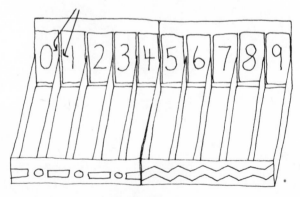

CIGAR BOXES

82

PLAYING THE NUMBER GAME. The 45 ice-cream sticks correspond to the quantitative total of the ten divisions of the number box: $0 + 1 + 2 + 3 + 4 + 5 + 6 + 7 + 8 + 9 = 45$. Keep the 45 sticks in a separate little box beside the number box. Begin by putting one stick in the number 1-section, then two sticks in the 2-section, etc., until there are nine left to place in the 9-section. If nine are not left for the last section, or if any sticks remain after the nine sections have been filled, there is an error somewhere. Now have your child distribute the 45 sticks herself. Many children will want to put some sticks into the 0-section: emphasize that this division is zero and gets none. Point out also that the little box containing the 45 sticks is now empty—that it is like the 0-section when it has none. After the game is finished, encourage your child to replace all the sticks into this little box for the next time she wants to play. When your child is proficient at this exercise, you may invent your own variations on the numbers game.

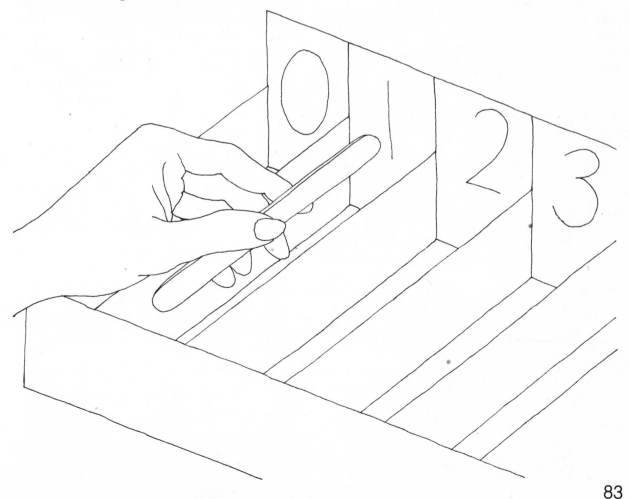

# Chapter 20: Number Rods

In the previous play-exercise, the value of numbers was demonstrated by counting actual, representative quantities. Here the value of numbers is approached in a relative, rather than absolute, sense. The different digits are represented by proportionately sized number rods. These comprise a sequence of size gradation to show the numerical progression 1-2-3-4-5-6-7-8-9-10. The colorful, attractive rods provide a tangible method for visualizing and teaching the simplest arithmetic relationships: for example, that 4 is twice as large as 2, or that 1 + 6 is the same as 3 + 4.

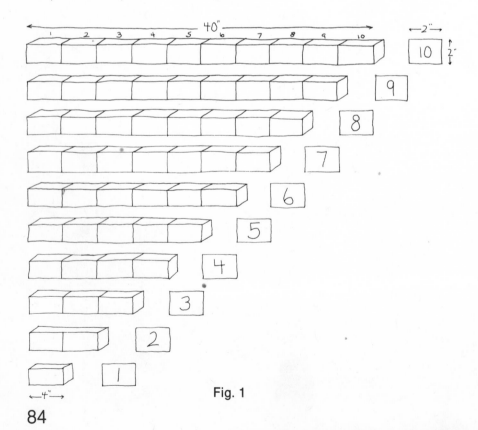

Fig. 1

Fig. 2

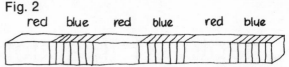

red  blue  red  blue  red  blue

MAKING THE RODS. To make the rods you will need somewhat less than 24 feet of wood. Ask for four 6' or three 8' lengths of one-by-one (1" x 1") at the lumber yard, or at a large hardware or household supply store that carries wood molding. ½" x ¾" molding will serve just as well at a slightly less expense. If you wish to avoid working with wood, you may use strips of rigid cardboard instead (although you will be sacrificing the third dimension and the durability of the toy). The number rods should be constructed according to the scale 1 unit = 4": thus the 10-rod is 40", the 9-rod 36", etc. (see Fig. 1). Once you have made the rods, forget about their actual lengths; the exercise is

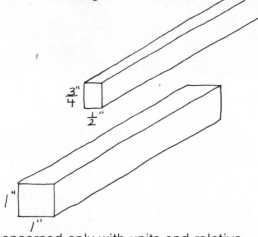

concerned only with units and relative lengths. Make sure your cuts are precise (a small handsaw or coping saw is recommended). When the ten rods are cut to size, and their rough edges finished with sandpaper, use a yardstick and pencil to mark off the unit divisions at 4" intervals. Also make ten cardboard squares, 2" x 2", each bearing one of the numbers from 1-10.

The unit divisions on all the rods should be painted in either of two ways. (1) An odd-even pattern: paint all odd-numbered units red, for example, and all the even units blue. This pattern (Fig. 2) works well for older children. (2) A multi-colored pattern works better for younger children: the first unit on all the rods is painted red; the second unit, blue; the third, green; fourth, white; fifth, brown; sixth, yellow; seventh, purple; eighth, gray; ninth, orange; tenth, black. See Figure 1. The multi-color pattern can be done very neatly with 10 different enamel paints and strips of masking tape to help keep a straight line between unit colors. Or, at considerably

less expense, you may use a multi-colored set of children's paints and a small brush.

WORKING WITH THE NUMBER RODS. On a table or the floor arrange the ten rods as in Figure 1. Place the 2" x 2" number squares beside the rods. The sequence is from large to small. Describe the arrangement to your child, emphasizing the correspondence between length and number. "This is the longest rod," you might say, "it is the 10-rod because it has ten sections." Point out the 1-rod, the shortest. Then describe the others in the sequence. Have your child run his hands along each of the rods to "feel" its length. When he is familiar with the idea of ten different size rods, corresponding to the ten numbers, you should begin to describe the colored units on the rods. Have him count the sections on the 10-rod first; then do the others. If you are using a multi-colored set, expalin the color relationships among the numbers from rod to rod. Point out the alternation of red and blue sections if you are using that pattern. In this regard, you might offer some comment on the concept of odd and even numbers. Illustrate the former with the red units and the latter with the blue divisions on the number rods.

Try some arithmetic exercises by moving the rods about. Demonstrate, for example, that 2 + 5 = 7 by making two equal lengths from the three rods. To these you may add

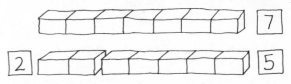

the combined 6-rod and 1-rod, and the combined 3-rod and 4 rod, to show two more ways of making seven. Adding with the number rods can be demonstrated with great variety. Subtraction exercises are similar. Put a 4-rod and a 1-rod together, parallel with the 5-rod, and ask your child to subtract 1 from 5. After he removes the 1-rod, the answer may be confirmed by counting the units on the remaining 4-rod. There are many possible ways of using the number rods for simple arithmetic exercises. Your child, like the children in my classroom, will surely come up with some ideas of his own.

# Chapter 21: Fraction Disks

Jennifer is eating a pizza that is divided into eight equal slices. She knows that one piece has been eaten, but she does not understand your meaning if you tell her that **one eighth** of the pizza is gone. The meaning of a fraction is difficult for a child to conceptualize. The play-exercises in this chapter use circular cut-outs to illustrate tangibly the parts of the whole. These fraction disks concretely demonstrate the proportionate sizes of eighths, sixths, fourths, thirds, and halves, in relation to a uniform whole. Figure 1 shows the six fraction disks, with the eighths-disk represented in actual size.

MAKING THE DISKS. The disks will be made out of posterboard; a heavier, corrugated cardboard should be used for backing the circular frames. About 12″ of wooden dowel (⅜″ diameter) will be needed for making the small pick-up knobs. Necessary tools include a compass, protractor (or a triangle measure for 60° and 45°), scissors, razor knife, and glue. Begin by making six squares of posterboard, measuring 6″ x 6″ each, and six squares of corrugated cardboard of the same dimension. The disks themselves, 5″ in diameter, will be cut out of the posterboard. Locate the center point of each posterboard square by intersecting two diagonals. With the compass set on this point of intersection,

draw a circle of 2½″ radius.

Figure 2 shows the division of the circles into the fractional components. For the halves-disk, simply draw a diameter. The quadrants of the fourths-disk are already outlined by the two intersecting diagonals of the square. For the eighths-disk, draw two perpendicular diameters at 45° from the original diagonals. Draw the thirds-disk by making three 120° sections, and outline the sixths-disk by halving the sections of the thirds-disk into six 60° sections. Diagramming the parts of the disks should be done with accuracy, since they will be interchanged during the exercises: that is, one section of the halves-disk must equal two parts of the fourths-disk, etc. Cut the fully diagrammed disk out of the posterboard, as in Figure 3. Glue the remaining circular frames to the 6″ x 6″ corrugated cardboard backing. Now cut up the five fraction disks (excluding the whole-disk) into their outlined sections. You should obtain 23 pieces, plus the whole disk. Cut 24 knobs, about ⅜″-½″ each, from the piece of wooden dowel (Fig. 4). Glue them on to the fraction-pieces, making handles like those used for the geometric insets.

LEARNING ABOUT FRACTIONS. While your child is learning the names and proportions of the various fractions, she is

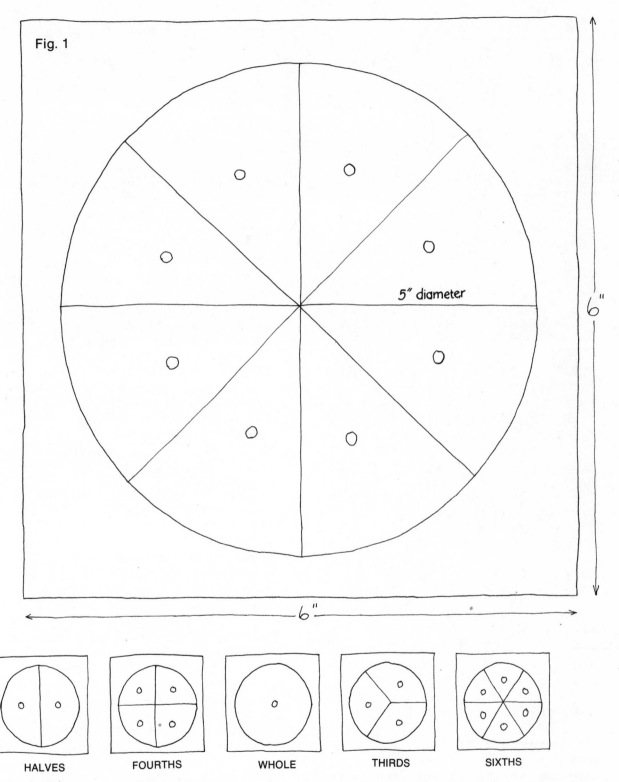

**Fig. 1**

5″ diameter

6″

6″

| HALVES | FOURTHS | WHOLE | THIRDS | SIXTHS |

also continuing to develop the three-fingered sense by manipulating the pick-up knobs. Make sure you encourage her to hold the knobs properly if she is not doing so. Begin these play-exercises by familiarizing your child with the names of the fractions. Say, for example, "this is the disk with two sections, called halves," or, "this is the disk with six sections, called sixths," etc. Have her count the six pieces in the sixths-disk, and all the parts of the other disks as well.

Fig. 2

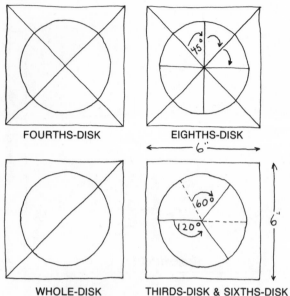

FOURTHS-DISK      EIGHTHS-DISK

WHOLE-DISK      THIRDS-DISK & SIXTHS-DISK
& HALVES-DISK

Once she has been introduced to the names of the fractions, follow the three-point method for helping her to learn them. Isolate two disks, the fourths and the halves, for example. (1) Take one fourth out from the fourths-disk, place it before her, and say, "this is a fourth." Do the same with a half-piece from the halves-disk. (2) Now ask your child to show you a fourth, and then a half. (3) When she does this correctly, point again to the half and ask, "what is this called?" If she makes a mistake, go over the whole procedure again.

Fig. 3

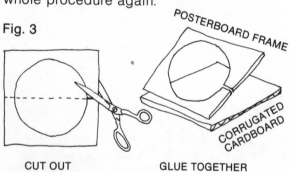

CUT OUT      GLUE TOGETHER

After your child has learned the single-fraction names—one-half, one-fourth, etc—this method can be used to teach her the names of the multi-fractions, for example, seven-eighths, three-fourths, five-sixths, etc. Have her examine the fourths-disk and count its parts. Remove one of the sections and point to the area covered by the three pieces remaining. Let your child

Fig. 4

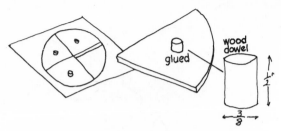

count these pieces, and see now if she fully understands the meaning of the fraction three-fourths. For later play-exercises, you can describe and illustrate the extent to which the fraction disks have interchangeable parts. Show your child how the half-piece will completely occupy the space of three sixth-pieces, two-fourths, etc. on the other disks. Show her how two eighth-pieces will fit into the space of one fourth, how two sixth-pieces will occupy the space of one third. On the other hand, certain pieces will not fit with certain others in a circular frame: for example, two third-pieces and one half-piece cannot occupy a single disk. Of course, there are many combinations to play with using these fraction disks, though it is best to concentrate on just two or three disks at the beginning.

# Chapter 22: Number Boards

After your child has learned to count to ten, the sequence from 11 to 99 will present a much greater challenge. But the challenge need not be so great as it seems. Built into our counting system is a concept that makes the higher numbers, say 23 or 78, meaningful to your child in terms of what he already knows about the first ten numbers. These, he will learn, are part of a numerical system based on a pattern of repeating tens. A child who is not being consciously guided by the base-ten concept might find his rambling through the higher numbers to be a stumbling and erratic experience. The point of this chapter is to make the base-ten concept accessible to your child and to demonstrate, in a tangible way, just how it operates: how the pattern of ten is repeated in conjunction with the digits which he has already mastered, so that the sequence 30-39, for example, can be as readily grasped as the digital sequence 0-10. The concept is taught by using two number boards: one is specifically designed to illustrate the formation of the numbers 11-19, the other to illustrate 19-99.

MAKING THE NUMBER BOARDS AND COMPONENTS. The base-ten concept will be concretely illustrated by a bundle of ten ice-cream sticks (or the like), held together by a rubber band. Individual digits from 1-9 are represented by a corresponding number of separate sticks. In all, 135 sticks will be needed to carry out the exercises. Have a dozen small rubber bands available. Beside these, you will need two small pieces of cardboard: one scrap of posterboard (no less than 3″ x 4″), and one of heavy carton-thickness (no less than 4″ x 11″). Make the number boards by cutting the heavier cardboard into two rectangular pieces, each 11″ x 2″ (Fig. 1). At one-inch intervals on each of the number boards, draw a **thick** line, about ⅛″ wide, brightly

Fig. 1

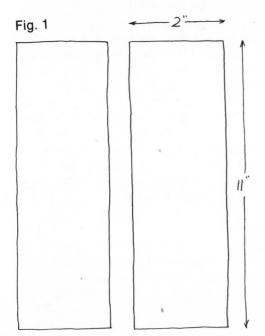

Fig. 2

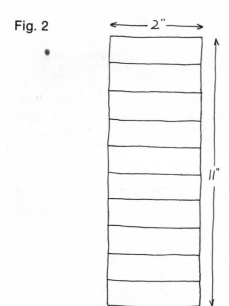

colored, using paint or felt tip pen (see Fig. 2). Thus you will actually be drawing nine horizontal lines, dividing the board into ten one-inch sections. (The combined thickness of the nine lines, about one inch, accounts for the overall length of the eleven-inch number board.) Now, as in Figure 3, write the number 10 in all but the bottom of the spaces on the first number board: this is Board I. Similarly, write the numbers 10, 20, 30. . . 90 within the spaces of the second board: Board II. Note the blank section on the bottom of each board.

Fig. 3

| BOARD I | BOARD II |
|---------|----------|
| 10 | 10 |
| 10 | 20 |
| 10 | 30 |
| 10 | 40 |
| 10 | 50 |
| 10 | 60 |
| 10 | 70 |
| 10 | 80 |
| 10 | 90 |
|  |  |

Using the posterboard, now make eleven one-inch squares (Fig. 4). Write one of the digits on each, making two with zero (0). These squares will be referred to as the number cards. Finally, make nine bundles of ice-cream sticks—ten sticks per bundle —bound together by a rubber band (Fig 5). The remaining sticks should be kept in a loose pile, from which they will be taken for individual use during the play-exercises.

Fig. 4

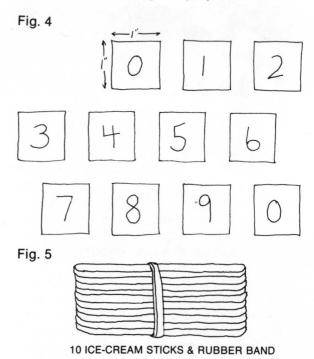

Fig. 5

**10 ICE-CREAM STICKS & RUBBER BAND**

COUNTING WITH THE NUMBER BOARDS. Prepare the counting game by first lining up the number cards from 0 to 9 (the second zero will be used later). Stack the sticks in nine, neatly bound bundles. Have your child count, and then compare, ten loose sticks with each bundle. The point is to be sure that he fully comprehends what each bundle represents: the base-ten concept. The first phase of the number exercises, involving only Board I, concretely teaches the counting process from 11 to 19. All 135 sticks will be used (note that 11 + 12 + 13 + 14 + 15 + 16 + 17 + 18 + 19 = 135).

With Figure 6 as a guide, begin by placing one bundle of sticks next to the uppermost 10 on the board. The written number 10 is thus tangibly illustrated. Now take the number card 1 and place it over the zero; place one loose stick next to the bundle. 11

is produced. Tell your child that eleven **is** ten plus one. Explain to him just what you have done with the sticks and the number card. Have him count all the sticks. This process, in essence, will be used throughout.

Fig. 6

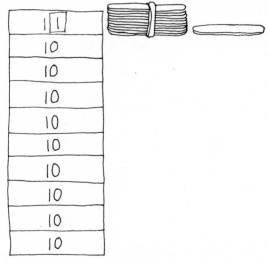

Now, in a vertical column, place the remaining eight bundles next to the other 10's on Board I. Place two loose sticks across from the second 10, and cover its zero with the number card 2. Again, have your child count the sticks, and now point to the 12 which appears on the number board. Proceed in this manner until you reach 19 (Fig. 7). Younger children (3-5½ yrs.) may

Fig. 7

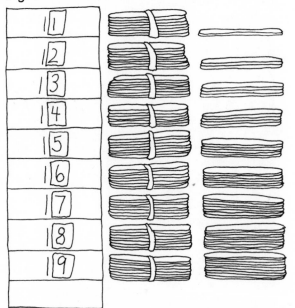

not reach 19 overnight: 14 or 15 would be a good day's work for them. But not until your child has mastered 11-19 should you introduce the second number board.

Board II introduces the numbers 20-99. But the transition from 19 to 20 is made, first, by utilizing the blank section at the bottom of Board I. Make this transition by repeating the last part of the previous exercise, producing 19 with the sticks and the number card. Tell your child that after nineteen comes twenty. Demonstrate this by adding another stick to the loose pile of nine, making two groups of ten; move these twenty sticks down one space, across from the bank section. Now place a 2 card in the tens column, and a 0 card in the digit column, demonstrating that here are 2 tens only, just as the sticks indicate (Fig. 8). Say to your child, "this is

Fig. 8

BOARD I

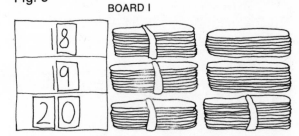

twenty." Transfer the 9 card and nineteen sticks to the top section of Board II (see Fig. 9). Below these, put two ten-bundles across from the 20 section. Board II operates by placing the number cards over the zeros in the digit column, and adding the appropriate number of loose sticks to the

Fig. 9    BOARD II

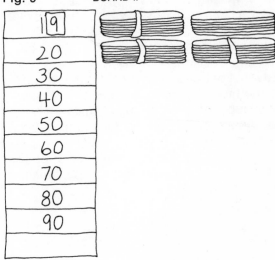

bundles. When ten loose sticks are collected, they are replaced by a ten-bundle.

Beginning with 20, it should no longer be necessary to count all the sticks in the ten-bundles. Your child now understands that 2 tens represent twenty sticks. Take him through the twenties as you did through the teens. When you get to 29, add one more loose stick, exchange the ten loose ones for one bundle, and move the three bundles down to the 30 section on the board. Teach your child the names twenty, thirty, forty, etc. When counting, say, to 56, he need only count 5 tens and then 6 single sticks, saying the final number "fifty-six" (see Fig. 10).

**Fig. 10**

Getting from 19 to 30 is a big accomplishment, and might require a long period of time. Surely days, possibly weeks, will be needed to complete all these play-exercises. Your child should not be rushed. Your patience will be to his advantage in learning the numbers. While 99 is the last number in the game, you may introduce the idea of 100 by using ten ten-bundles and placing the 1 card with the two 0 cards on the bottom section of Board II. Note, however, that your child will probably not feel at all uncomfortable about finishing with the number 99.

# Chapter 23: Beads and Cards

Using the number rods and number boards in previous chapters, your child has come to terms with the basics of counting and the simplest of addition and subtraction problems. With the use of different materials, this chapter enables your child to work out arithmetic operations involving three-digit numbers. Completing these exercises is a long process, needless to say: most children will master only the basic principles in the early lessons. But I am sure you will be surprised to see how quickly children can learn to grasp and manipulate big numbers. Arithmetic involving numbers in the hundreds requires, essentially, no more than the ability to count to ten and an understanding of the base-ten concept of our number system. With this knowledge, your child is fully equipped to add 258 to 677. What is needed are the means for making these large numbers less threatening to your child and more readily accessible in concrete terms. These are provided by the beads and cards in the following play-exercises.

ORGANIZING THE MATERIALS. Arithmetic computation—adding or subtracting—is a simplified way of counting. The simplicity of the process may be illustrated by using wooden or plastic beads to represent the numbers concretely. Small cards with numbers written on them are used for abstract representation of the tangible quantities. The beads and cards are used together to teach addition and subtraction.

1. **Beads**. You will need approximately 200 beads, all the same size, about ¼″-⅜″ in diameter (it would be a good idea to obtain a handful more than you need, to ensure against loss or breakage). These can be purchased inexpensively at any crafts or 5 & 10¢ store. Also obtain some strong thread—nylon or carpet thread. The beads will be grouped in three ways: as units, as 10-strings, and as 100-squares. (a) Set aside eighteen beads to be used individually as **unit-beads**. (b) Make eighteen strings of 10 beads each, carefully knotting the two ends to keep these **10-strings** intact. (c) The **100-squares** are made not actually with the beads, but by drawing a hundred little circles on a small piece of square cardboard. These circles should be the same size as the actual beads, so that the square itself will measure 10 beads x 10 beads. Thus for ⅜″ beads, the square will be 3¾″ x 3¾″. Make eighteen of these 100-squares. See Figure 1. Keep the unit-beads, the 10-strings, and the 100-squares in a box or tray which may be referred to as the "bank."

2. **Cards**. The number cards, easily made by cutting 3″ x 5″ index cards, are

## Fig. 1

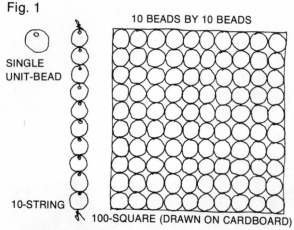

SINGLE
UNIT-BEAD

10 BEADS BY 10 BEADS

10-STRING

100-SQUARE (DRAWN ON CARDBOARD)

correspondingly grouped in three sets. (a) Cut eighteen cards measuring 1½″ x 3″. Write the numbers 1-9 on these cards, so that threre are two cards bearing each number. (b) For the second set, cut eighteen cards measuring 3″ x 3″. Make two for each of the numbers 10, 20, 30 . . . 90. (c) The third set consists of two cards each for the numbers 100, 200, 300 . . . 900, written on eighteen cards cut to 4½″ x 3″. See Figure 2. This

## Fig. 2

1½″ (ACTUAL SIZE)

3″

1″max.

NUMBER CARDS

4½″

3″

1½ - 1½ - 1½

3″

1½″

600 + 20 + 7

627 → 627

94

makes 54 cards in all, three sets of eighteen. Since these cards will be superimposed over one another to illustrate various numbers, each digit should be written uniformly to occupy about one inch of space across the card, or part of the card, that bears it. Figure 2 illustrates how the number 627 is made by superimposing a 7-card over a 20-card over a 600-card.

WORKING WITH THE BEADS: THE IDEA OF EXCHANGE. The first phase of the play-exercise is designed to illustrate a basic principle operating in the computation of many simple arithmetic problems. In the case of addition, it is the principle of "carrying over" tens (or hundreds) from one column to the next: "borrowing" tens is the analagous process in subtraction. In these play-exercises, both processes—borrowing and carrying—are indicated by the single term "exchange." The concept of exchange may be concretely presented in the following way. Line up ten **unit-beads** and ask your child to count them. Beside these place one **10-string**. Take the time to demonstrate that each 10-string is the same length as the ten unit-beads. Have your child count the beads on a few of the 10-strings. Make the point that every time ten unit-beads are collected, they can be replaced by one 10-string (or vice versa). This is called **exchange**. (See Fig. 3.) Explain that 2 tens

## Fig. 3—"EXCHANGE"

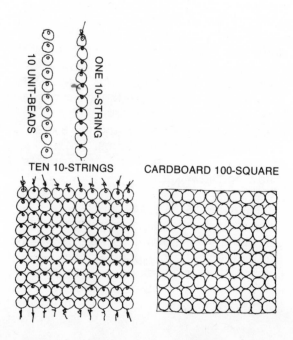

10 UNIT-BEADS

ONE 10-STRING

TEN 10-STRINGS

CARDBOARD 100-SQUARE

are called twenty, 3 tens thirty, and so on until ninety. Once she fully understands that one 10-string is interchangeable with ten units, because they represent equal quantities, introduce the idea that ten 10-strings are equal to one **100-square**. As in Figure 3, line up ten rows of 10-strings beside one 100-square. Have your child count the strings, and ten count the ten rows of beads drawn on the square. Again, make the point that ten 10-strings can be exchanged for one 100-square. Explain that 10 tens are called one-hundred, that 2 100-squares represent the number two-hundred, that 3 hundreds are called three-hundred, etc., until nine-hundred. Exchange usually proves to be an easy concept for children to grasp if you are careful to line up the unit-beads, or 10-strings, **neatly** beside the sets that they equal.

ADDITION. Begin the addition exercises by using beads from the bank. Practice exchange with the example, say, of 4 + 7, or 9 + 2. Have your child count out 4 beads, then 7 beads, and line them all up. Then ask her to count the sum of these beads and remind her to exchange 10 unit beads for one 10-string. She will be left with one 10-string and one unit-bead, a sum of eleven. Similarly, she may practice

exchange by adding 80 + 50. Ask her to make one group of eight 10-strings, and one group of five 10-strings (Fig. 4). Let her put both groups together and count the total number of strings. Now, ask her what she is supposed to do with ten of these 10-strings. She should exchange them for a 100-square from the bank. Then she will have one square and three strings, or one hundred and three tens. Tell her the name of this new sum: one hundred and thirty.

So far she has been dealing with the numbers as tangible quantities. The names for these numbers are indicated on the cards. Introduce the cards and tell her the names that each one represents. Now you may go back to the previous example to show how the beads and cards may be used together. Bring out an 80-card and a 50-card, and ask her first to get 80 beads from the bank, and then 50 beads. If she has trouble, explain again that 80 is the name for eight 10-strings, and 50 the name for five. Ask her to group the strings separately, now under the appropriate number cards (as in Fig. 4), and then put them together to make the exchange. When the exchange has been made, leaving one 100-square and three 10-strings, place down two new cards (a 100-card and a 30-card) to label the rearranged beads. Now place another

Fig. 4

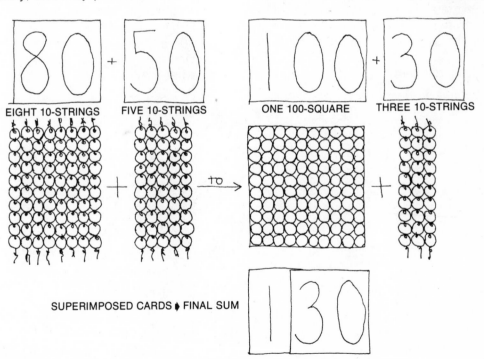

SUPERIMPOSED CARDS ♦ FINAL SUM

30-card on top of another 100-card as in Figure 4. Tell your child that the cards name the groups of beads and help us to remember how many have been counted.

Continue with the addition of numbers such as 264 + 329, 107 + 95, 243 + 515. The only limitation on your choice of example problems is the need to keep the final sum below 1000, since the cards you have made

Fig. 5

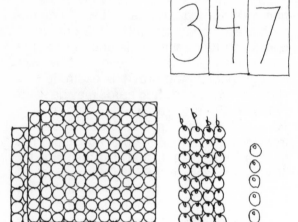

go no higher than 999. In all the problems, remind your child to make the necessary exchanges before reading out the answer. When requesting a specific number of beads for an addition problem, pick out and arrange the appropriate number cards for each of the addends. Superimpose, for example, three cards to make the number

347 and ask your child to collect the beads for that number. Should she have difficulty, take apart the cards to indicate precisely what is needed: seven unit-beads for the 7-card, four 10-strings for the 40-card, and three 100-squares for the 300-card (see Fig. 5). Be deliberate in starting with the units, next the tens, and finally the hundreds. Keep the beads arranged neatly under the cards. Remember that all the arithmetic operations are performed by manipulating the beads, and that the cards are used only to name the numbers.

SUBTRACTION. Subtraction problems merely reverse the above procedures. Your child will probably find these exercises somewhat easier. Present the number cards for 786 and ask her to get that many beads from the bank. Then ask her to take away 421 of these beads and place them in another area. IMPORTANT: Remind her to subtract, first from the units, then from the tens, and finally from the hundreds. Now ask her to label the 421 subtracted beads with the number cards. Next, she should count what remains in the original group: there will be five unit-beads, six 10-strings, and three 100-squares. This remainder should be labeled 365 with the cards. It does not matter greatly if she has mis-counted and made a mistake. If, for example, she has counted 265 instead of 365, give her the 200-card, the 60-card, and the 5-card to label her answer. Understanding the method in general is what really matters. Confidence is most

Fig. 6 BEFORE SUBTRACTION & AFTER EXCHANGE

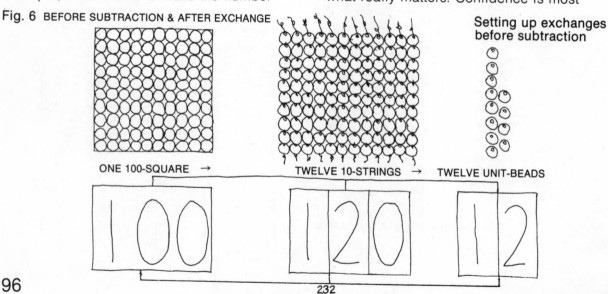

ONE 100-SQUARE →     TWELVE 10-STRINGS →     TWELVE UNIT-BEADS

Setting up exchanges before subtraction

232

important at first; accuracy will come with practice.

The example 786 minus 421 does not require borrowing, or exchange. Introduce the exchange concept in subtraction with the example 232 minus 195. Use the regular procedure for grouping and labeling the two numbers. Remind your child to begin subtracting in the units column. When she realizes that she cannot take away five beads from two, remind her about exchange. 232 is represented by two 100-squares, three 10-strings, and two unit-beads. Point out that one of the 10-strings can be exchanged for ten unit-beads from the bank. Now she can subtract 5 units from 12 units, leaving 7. At this point she is left with two 10-strings, from which nine must be taken away. Have her replace one of the 100-squares with ten 10-strings. Now she can subtract 9 strings from 12, leaving 3. Finally, there is one remaining 100-square, from which one other 100-square must be taken away. Since no squares will be left, the final answer is represented by the three strings and seven beads. Label the result with the number cards, a 7-card superimposed on a 30-card. The exchange of one 100-square for ten 10-strings, and one 10-string for ten units, can be fully represented before the actual taking-away operations are begun. The necessary rearrangement of the grouping of the 232 beads for performing this operation is thus represented in Figure 6. Use the number cards to label each step of the operation. Change the cards as your child performs each part of the subtraction exercise. Soon she will be able to label the beads by herself. Then all you will have to do is suggest addition and subtraction problems. Your child will do the rest.

# Part V: Language

The purpose of these chapters is to orient your child to the written language as an extension of the spoken word. Words are associated with representational objects, and then presented as phonetic units. Pronouncing these units involves combining the common phonetic sounds of the individual letters. In Part V your child will also enjoy playing with boxes and cards that serve to teach some important grammatical distinctions.

# Chapter 24: Phonetic Word Cards—Part 1

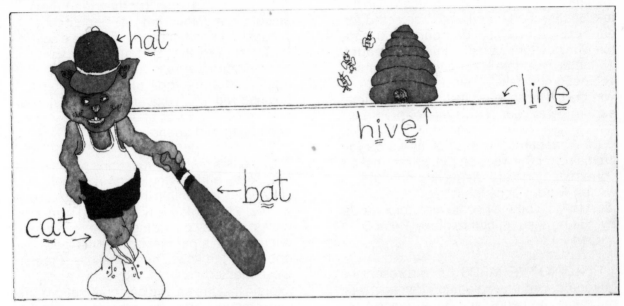

With the sandpaper letters, your child was introduced to the most common sounds of the individual letters of the alphabet. This chapter presents a systematic introduction to the reading and pronunciation of individual words. Since the spoken language translates letter symbols into phonetic sounds—that is, since we communicate phonetically—it must be stressed that the term **reading** in this chapter is nearly synonymous with **pronouncing**. If a child perceives that the word "hug" conveys the sound "huge"—which would be a logical perception based on a purely literal understanding of the alphabet—he would not be able to communicate his meaning. In reading, then, as in speaking, the words must be perceived phonetically; there must be a kind of internal pronunciation which enables the child to correlate the written with the spoken word. The underlying principle in this chapter is to illustrate this correlation.

The system is based on the phonetic values of the letter-symbols. Because the English vowels, and vowel combinations, vary widely in their pronunciation, the example words in this chapter illustrate the vowel sounds that most commonly occur in a child's vocabulary. Needless to say, there will be many common words that will not be taken into account; for simplicity's sake, this approach to reading is highly selective and makes no pretense to including the full range of sounds that your child uses in his everyday speech. Specifically, eleven sounds—among those presented in the Montessori method—will be the focus in the following play-exercises. These sounds may be grouped under three headings: (1) single vowels—**a**, **e**, **i**, **o**, **u**; (2) combined vowels (or diphthongs)—**ai**, **ea**, **ee**, **oo**; (3) the "silent **e**"—how the final, unpronounced **e** affects the pronunciation of **a** and **i**, for example.

PREPARING THE MATERIALS. The method involves a presentation of short words together with pictures illustrating those words. Everything may be conveniently presented on 3″ x 5″ index cards; about 200 of them will be necessary. Three groups of cards should be made:

(1) Letter cards. On each of eleven cards, simply write one of the eleven letters, or letter combinations, named above: **a**, **e**, **i**, **o**, **u**, **ai**, **ea**, **ee**, **oo**, **a—e**, **i—e** (see Fig. 1).

(2) Word-picture cards. Refer to the **Table of Suggested Words**. From each column, representing one phonetic sound, select from five to eight words. Choose words that

you can conveniently illustrate with small magazine or newspaper pictures, photos, or with drawings of your own. As in Figure 2, write the word with its accompanying illustration pasted on the index card. Do this to illustrate the several words selected for each of the eleven sounds. Your may arrange the word-picture cards in columns, headed by the appropriate letter card. (Of course, you need not make all eleven sets at once; you may choose to do just a few at a time, according to your child's rate of progress.)

(3) Word cards. For each of the words you are using for the word-picture cards, make a corresponding card displaying only the written word. (Since these require no illustration, you may conserve index cards by cutting them in half to make 1½" x 5" pieces.)

READING THE CARDS. As you present the materials, certain explanatory remarks will, of course, be necessary. But a general, ordered procedure can be used for introducing all the sounds. (1) Start with a letter card, and refresh your child's memory about phonetic pronunciation. The letter **a**, for example, is pronounced "ah" like in **cat**. Have him pronounce this sound of the letter **a**. (2) With the **a** letter card, present the word-picture card for **cat**. (3) Explain that the **a** in the word **cat** is pronounced "ah"; ask him to read the word by pronouncing separately all the letters in the word: "kuh"(**c**)-"ah"(**a**)-"tuh"(**t**): then read them smoothly, together, **cat**. (4) Repeat the process for another example of the **a** sound. (5) Do at least five, and align the word-picture cards in a column, with the letter card at the top. (6) When you have finished with each example sound, ask your child if he can think of other words containing that sound.

Using this method, your child will learn to read, first, all the single vowel sounds and the words that contain them. The illustrations will help to reinforce his learning of the written word by providing a concrete, visual reference. In a parallel fashion, he may now approach the vowel combinations. Present these methodically as suggested above. Explain that the **ee** and **ea** combinations are both pronounced in the same way: like in the word **sea** or **weed**. The **ai** sound is pronounced like in the word **hair**. Some difficulty may arise when you get to the **oo** combination, because this diphthong has two equally common pronunciations in the child's everyday vocabulary. Explain the need for making two columns now, because

## TABLE OF SUGGESTED WORDS

| a | e | i | o | u | ai | ea | ee | oo (long) | oo (abrupt) |
|---|---|---|---|---|----|----|----|-----------|-------------|
| hat | red | lip | top | cup | sail | bead | jeep | moon | foot |
| bat | hen | bib | mop | bus | hair | tea | heel | pool | wood |
| cat | men | rib | mom | tub | pail | ear | reel | root | book |
| dad | leg | pin | pot | nut | air | meat | seed | loop | wool |
| rag | pen | pig | dot | hut | fair | sea | feet | boot | hook |
| bag | web | kid | fox | mud | mail | eat | beet | food | cook |
| man | jet | fig | box | sun | lair | seal | peel | tool | hood |
| rat | egg | six | log | bun | rail | seam | weed | room | soot |
| tap | net | fin | cot | gun | hail | beak | reef | broom | brook |
| mat | ten | mint | doll | cub | jail | pea | keel | hoop | rook |

| | | | i—e | a—e | | | | | |
|---|---|---|-----|-----|---|---|---|---|---|
| | | | five | cake | | | | | |
| | | | pine | lake | | | | | |
| | | | fire | page | | | | | |
| | | | kite | gate | | | | | |
| | | | line | snake | | | | | |
| | | | pipe | cage | | | | | |
| | | | hive | tape | | | | | |
| | | | tile | ape | | | | | |
| | | | file | face | | | | | |
| | | | mice | lace | | | | | |

**Fig. 1** LETTER CARDS

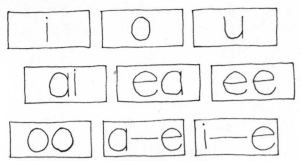

| i | o | u |
| ai | ea | ee |
| oo | a–e | i–e |

**oo** may stand for either the long sound in **food** or the abrupt sound in **book**. Over-emphasize the longness, or the abruptness, when demonstrating these sounds for your child. For the **oo** words the pictures—representing words which have long been a part of his speaking vocabulary—will be especially valuable in

**Fig. 2**

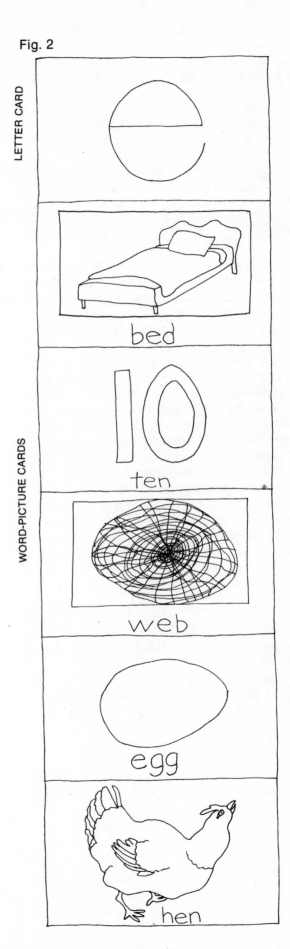

LETTER CARD

e

WORD-PICTURE CARDS

bed

ten

web

egg

hen

**Fig. 3**

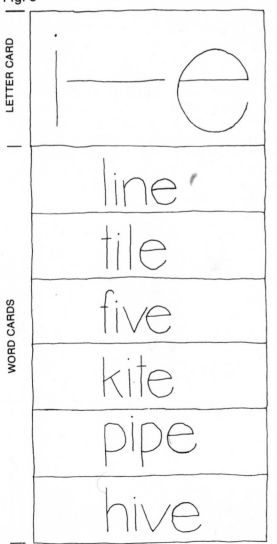

LETTER CARD

i—e

WORD CARDS

line

tile

five

kite

pipe

hive

helping him to memorize which of them are read like **food**, and which like **book**.

Introduce the **a—e** and **i—e** combinations by explaining the silent **e**: usually **e**, at the end of a word, is not pronounced at all. But when there is a silent **e**, as in **cake** or **tile**, the preceding vowel is lengthened, that is, it is pronounced just as it would be in the alphabet song. Again, use the columns of word-picture cards to accustom your child to this peculiarity of pronunciation. Actually, teaching these long vowel sounds, with the examples of **a** and **i**, is your child's first formal introduction to the idea that the vowels may be pronounced in more than one way. Emphasize this by comparing **pin**, for example, to **pine**, or **tap** to **tape**.

When your child has mastered the single and combined vowel sounds, and is able to read the words presented on the word-picture cards, he is ready to try reading the words without the help of concrete, visual reference. This is, perhaps, the most difficult and significant step in the learning-to-read process. Now, as in Figure 3, arrange columns beginning with the letter card and including at least five examples of the words with which he is already familiar from the earlier phase of the play-exercises. Ask your child to read the words from the plain word cards. If he should have trouble, you may then present the corresponding word-picture card for help.

Besides being instructive, these play-exercises can truly be appreciated as delightful games for your child. Arranging the cards themselves, the pictures, the acts of repetition and imitation, and the great satisfaction of discovery and success—all provide good fun while introducing your child to one of the most important areas of his education.

# Chapter 25: Phonetic Cards—Part 2

The following play-exercises continue to develop your child's basic reading skills with the addition of some new sounds. Emphasis in this chapter is on special consonant combinations, and on some selected vowel-consonant combinations. The sounds to be studied now, like those before, are among those introduced in the Montessori classrooms. They are, of course, highly selective, chosen for either their frequency of occurrence in common words or their special uniqueness. You may find it appropriate to introduce other letter combinations of your own choosing.

MAKING THE PHONETIC CARDS. Twelve combinations and the letter **y** are suggested here. Follow the general procedure described in the previous chapter. Make thirteen letter cards: **ar, er, ir, or, ur, ce, ck, sh, th, ch, ph, qu, y**. Have a few packs of 3″ x 5″ index cards available to make word cards illustrating the occurence of these combinations. A **Table of Suggested Words** is again provided, but you may certainly use any words to illustrate these sounds for your child. Since you cannot begin these play-exercises until your child has already developed a solid basis for phonetic comprehension, word-picture cards should not be necessary, although you may find them useful for some of the words. Illustrate the word cards, then, at your own discretion.

Note, however, that the **Table of Suggested Words** this time contains numerous words—abstract nouns, verbs, adjectives—that cannot be illustrated. Words that you choose for demonstrating a new sound should, for the most part, contain letters whose common sounds your child is already familiar with. **Ship**, for example, would be a good starter for the **sh** combination, since your child already knows the **i** and **p** sounds in that word; **she**, on the other hand, might be confusing because of the long **e**.

READING THE CARDS. Begin the play-exercises with one of the vowel-consonant combinations: **ar, er, ir, or**, or **ur**. Proceed to explain the sound and its relationship to the word in an orderly way. (1) Select a letter card. (2) Pronounce the sound. (3) Choose an example word card and pronounce the word. (4) Ask your child to "sound out" the new word, and then to pronounce it smoothly. (5) Demonstrate the new sound in this way with five to eight word cards, placed in a column under the letter card, as in Figure 1.

By introducing these combinations of r + the vowels, you are actually teaching your child new sounds for the vowels which she already knows in a certain way. Combination with **r** causes the vowel to be pronounced

Fig. 1

LETTER CARDS

WORD CARDS

differently. It is easier for her to grasp these new variations when presented in combination with the fixed consonant than it would be if the variant sounds were presented independently. For, in fact, all these combinations show a vowel pronunciation that is dependent on the r. When explaining these combinations, then, note that the **ar** is the sound in **arm**; it reveals a different **a** sound from the one in **cat**. Likewise, **er** reveals the sound of **e** in **her**, not in **pet**; and **or** illustrates the sound in **horn**. Note, and explain to your child, that **ir** and **ur** represent the same sound (**bird**, **curb**), and that this sound is basically the same as the **er** of **her**.

The other combinations will also require some explanation. The letter **c** can be pronounced either hard or soft. When **c** is followed by **e**, as in **rice**, it is a soft sound, the same as in **sun**. The hard sound always appears when **c** is combined with **k**, as in **neck**. Explain and pronounce the other combinations. **Sh** can appear at the beginning, middle, or end of a word (**ship**, **wish**, **fished**). The same is true for most of the others. The sounds made by **th** and **ch** can be felt on the tongue at the front and middle parts, respectively, of the mouth. **Qu**, like the **ck**, is felt at the back of the mouth. The **ph** sound is made just like the **f**.

## TABLE OF SUGGESTED WORDS

| ar | er | ir | or |
|---|---|---|---|
| arm | her | bird | worm |
| tar | camper | girl | cork |
| dart | herd | sir | horn |
| hard | butter | first | cord |
| far | sister | firm | lord |
| car | jerk | skirt | sport |
| star | term | mirth | for |
| farm | monster | stir | pork |
| park | faster | dirt | forget |
| dark | lobster | thirsty | storm |
| bark | older | twirl | short |
| carpet | fern | irk | work |

| ch | ck | sh | th |
|---|---|---|---|
| chin | duck | shop | that |
| chop | neck | short | think |
| charm | deck | fish | path |
| chug | clock | wash | three |
| lunch | lock | wish | this |
| much | sock | lash | then |
| chest | back | ship | thorn |
| such | stack | shape | them |
| chapel | rock | shake | Thelma |
| cheat | sick | ash | thing |
| finch | black | sharp | thumb |
| bench | pick | dish | bath |

| ce | ur | ph | qu |
|---|---|---|---|
| rice | burn | phone | quick |
| nice | hurt | telephone | quiet |
| mice | turn | graph | quill |
| lace | curb | telegraph | quit |
| space | curtain | Philip | quite |
| race | surf | elephant | squirt |
| trace | spurt | phrase | square |
| lance | curl | | |
| dance | occur | | |
| ice | hurl | | |
| ace | curd | | |
| fence | murmur | | |

| y (long i) | y (long e) |
|---|---|
| my | penny |
| by | funny |
| fly | mommy |
| cry | kitty |
| rely | Henry |
| sky | putty |
| try | twenty |
| dry | bunny |
| fry | empty |
| shy | silly |
| sly | furry |
| bye | sunny |

The letter y represents several sounds (**yes**, **system**, **mommy**, **fly**). Suggested for study here are the two contrasting sounds made by the letter y when it appears at the end of a word. Explain them as being like the sounds of the letters **e** and **i** in the alphabet song (long **e** and long **i**). Under the letter card make two columns to represent the two sounds (Fig. 2). Like in the previous exercises, work on one sound at a time. Place down one word card at a time and ask your child to pronounce the sounds in the word, and then the word itself.

Fig. 2

y

penny / sky
daddy / cry
kitty / try
twenty / shy
silly / bye

# Chapter 26: Singular and Plural

The concept of singular and plural is built into our language as it is in our perceptions. Understanding that language differentiates—and **how** language differentiates—between one of something and more-than-one of something, may give your child a secure feeling about the logical use of words. The simple play-exercises in this chapter approach the idea of singular and plural from a grammatical and, simultaneously, a representational (objective) point of view.

MAKING THE WORD-CARDS. The exercises employ word-cards and matching objects—small toys, common items, or magazine picture cut-outs. Cut some 3″ x 5″ index cards into rectangular pieces measuring 1″ x 3″. Make ten of these to begin with. Make also a one-inch square piece of cardboard, with the letter **s** written on it. On five of the 1″ x 3″ cards write (using lower case letters) the names of objects much as **cat, pin, dime, book, pen.** Leave enough space at the end of these singular word-cards for the square **s**-card to be added. On the five other cards, write the plurals of the words you have chosen: **cats, pins, dimes, books, pens.** The exercises call for some tangible representation of the words you have chosen. To illustrate the objects you need merely obtain four or five safety pins, about six dimes, a few small

books, and several pens. To illustrate **cat** in the singular, a magazine picture will do; for **cats,** a second picture, showing several cats (perhaps mother and kittens). For the purposes of these introductory play-exercises, be certain that the words you choose form their plurals by the simple addition of **-s.** (Words like fish, sheep, leaf, puppy, glass, fungus, etc. would obviously not be acceptable.)

PERCEIVING THE SINGULAR AND PLURAL. Do not be reluctant to use the terms 'singular' and 'plural' with your child. In fact, you may wish to make cards for those two words, to be used to head the two columns you will be working with. See Figure 2. Begin by vertically aligning the singular word-cards next to their corresponding objects (or pictures). Read aloud each word, from top to bottom, as you indicate the appropriate item to your child. When he understands the relationship between the object and the word, and grasps the idea of singularity, explain to him that more-than-one of any object will be indicated in the word by adding an **s.** This makes the word plural. To one of the singular words, then, add the square **s**-card and, simultaneously, introduce at least one more corresponding object (see Fig. 2).

Once your child understands the concept

**Fig. 1**

and the mechanics of plural formation, make a vertical column of all the plural word-cards. Opposite these place all their corresponding objects, except one, which should remain by the singular word, as in Figure 1. Now that you are using the plural word-cards, there is no further use for the square **s**-card. Read down the plural-word list, emphasizing the terminal **s** sound, while pointing out the several corresponding items. Soon your child will perceive the difference between, say, one pen and several pens, **on the written cards**. Try this experiment: gather up all the word-cards, but leave the one group of single objects and the other grouping of plural objects. Ask your child to match each of the ten word-cards with its appropriate object or grouping of objects.

For the next part of the play-exercise, gather up two or three sets of objects—say, 4 pens, 6 dimes, 3 pins—and have your child sort them into singular and plural distributions. The items should be arranged in six "piles": 3 pens, 1 pen, 5 dimes, 1 dime, 2 pins, 1 pin. Again, have him put the

appropriate word-card next to each item or group of items. Encourage your child, especially through your own actions, always to keep the singular and plural word-cards appropriately aligned and correspondent with the example objects. As your child progresses with these exercises, you may begin to add more word-cards and objects, as many as you think he can handle. Eventually, attempt using words without any corresponding objects. Simply ask your child if he can make the plural for the word **chair**, or the singular for **cars**.

**Fig. 2**

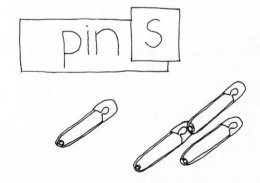

# Chapter 27: Noun-Box and Verb-Box

Does your child know that she can "jump" or "walk," but that she cannot "dime" or "leaf"? Or that she can see and touch a "pencil" but not a "write"? Unconsciously, of course, she has been aware of these differences for as long as she has been speaking. The noun-box and the verb-box are used in play-exercises designed to make children consciously aware of two basic parts of speech. Concrete terms and materials are employed in a logical method to help illustrate the simplest constructions of her language. By doing activities, and by the perception of things, your child can learn to conceptualize a distinction between words that function to describe her doing, and words that function to describe the objects of her perception. The concept "verb" is learned by association with her own activities in doing. "Noun" is presented concretely in association with objects she can see, touch, and handle.

PREPARING THE WORD-BOXES. Word-cards representing nouns and verbs will be contained within two boxes, the noun-box and the verb-box. Any two small cardboard boxes can be used for this purpose. If the boxes you obtain are the same color, paint one red and one blue. The red one should be labeled "nouns" on its lid, and the blue one labeled "verbs." If you cannot find two small boxes around the

house, you may make them out of cardboard, according to the directions given earlier for the sequence boxes. Or, you might even want to use the two largest sequence boxes, if you have already made them.

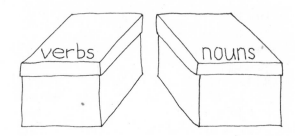

Next, you will need the word-cards. For the verb-box, cut 1″ x 3″ rectangles out of (preferably blue) 3″ x 5″ index cards. These will bear the verbal instructions. On each card write a simple action verb, for example, "run," "walk," "jump," "clap." Five or six should be enough to begin with. Consult the **Table of Suggested Words**. The noun-box

**Fig. 1**  CONTENTS OF THE NOUN-BOX

PLASTIC OBJECT

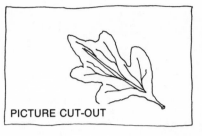

PICTURE CUT-OUT

WORD-CARD

will be used in three ways (see Fig. 1). First, consult the **Table**, and put in several 1″ x 3″ (preferably red) cards bearing object words, such as "jet," "leaf," "dime," "dog," "cone." Next, from a magazine make small picture cut-outs of noun-objects, such as "jet," "leaf," etc., and tape them onto red 1″ x 3″ cards. Finally, place some very small items—a dime, a tiny pine cone, a plastic dog—into the box with the other materials. It is helpful, but not necessary, to have correspondence among all the words, pictures, and objects in the noun-box.

LEARNING ABOUT NOUNS AND VERBS. It is best to begin with the noun-box. These play-exercises present the idea of noun through a logical method that proceeds from the tangible object itself to the symbolic word. Explain to your child that words denoting the names of objects are **nouns**. Illustrate this idea first with the small objects from the red box. Take them out, saying, "this is a dime—a dime is an object and the **word** dime is a noun"; "this is a cone," etc. Then point out objects around the room, emphasizing the noun as you name, for example, a book, a lamp, a banana, a plant, etc. Ask your child to identify other noun-objects in her environment. When she is familiar with them, show her the magazine pictures of objects. Explain how these cut-outs relate to the idea of nouns: remember, in this exercise you are dealing not with objects **per se**, but with objects **that are described by words called nouns**. Now show her the cards with the written words, "jet," "dime," etc. Use these cards to familiarize your child with the written and spoken word as a part of speech. Using the noun-box in these ways teaches the concept **noun** by demonstrating a progression from the concrete to the abstract.

If the noun-box is viewed as the object-box, its counterpart is the action-box.

Accordingly, this one has only words in it. Use five or six verb-cards to begin with. Familiarize your child with the words you have chosen. They should be verbs whose meanings are easily acted out, for example, walk, jump, hop, nod, stand, sit, clap, pat. Tell your child that these words are verbs, that they describe the action she does. If you choose the word-card "clap," have her clap as she reads the word. Let her sit, stand, scratch, etc., according to the instructions on the cards. Explain the difference between noun words and verb words by telling your child that she can **do** the verb words, but she cannot do the noun words. When she fully understands the distinction, mix the verb-cards with the noun-cards and ask her to sort them properly into the empty boxes. The color correspondence between the boxes and the cards will help your child to make her decisions. Once she is proficient at this, you may wish to obtain different boxes and make new word-cards without any color correspondences. Now you may have her sort the nouns from the verbs without the help of color associations.

| TABLE OF SUGGESTED WORDS | |
|---|---|
| verbs | nouns |
| run | leaf |
| walk | cone |
| sit | flower |
| stand | cup |
| hop | dime |
| jump | penny |
| clap | jet |
| pat | dog |
| wink | book |
| nod | table |
| kiss | shoe |
| smile | chair |
| blow | ear |
| draw | coat |
| write | candle |
| roll | television |
| eat | lamp |
| drink | tree |
| play | apple |
| dance | clock |

# Last Word

The American poet E. E. Cummings once wrote that "it takes three to make a child." Really, that's what **Child's Work** is all about. People getting together, big people (called parents) and little people (called children), to make things and do things for the sake of expanding through sharing and exploration. Many of the games in this book have called for careful measurements and detailed instructions. Hopefully, such concerns have not detracted from the vital spirit inherent in these pages—a spirit appealing to that indefinable sense of discovery which springs from growth like trees from roots. Children, the world's largest minority group, are the world's greatest artists, because they have not lost touch with the spontaneous vitality that the world at large continues to sap and drain out of taller people.

Maybe working with our children will help us to get back closer to our hidden, but ever present, childishness, to realize in fact that the child is the father of the man. This is something that cannot be measured, of course, as the true rewards of growth-in-process never can. It is time now to abandon the fantasy that children's activities can be measured at all. Let us welcome the more realistic view that growing up is something we know very little about—except that growing is living and that life can be the pure stuff of art. And "in so far as every child and woman and man may be immeasurable" (Cummings again) "art is the mystery of every man and woman and child." Perhaps **Child's Work** has made you feel some of that mystery.